D1717084

Insects, Spiders, and Creepy Crawlers

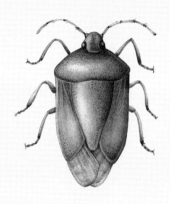

Insects, Spiders, and Creepy Crawlers

A supplement to
Childcraft—The How and Why Library

World Book, Inc.
a Scott Fetzer company
Chicago
www.worldbook.com

Staff

Vice President and Editor in Chief
Paul A. Kobasa

Editorial

Associate Director, Supplementary Publications
Scott Thomas

Managing Editor, Supplementary Publications
Barbara A. Mayes

Manager, Research, Supplementary Publications
Cheryl Graham

Senior Editor
Shawn Brennan

Permissions Editor
Janet T. Peterson

Manager, Indexing Services
David Pofelski

Administrative Assistant
Ethel Matthews

Graphics and Design

Associate Director
Sandra M. Dyrlund

Senior Designer
Don Di Sante

Photographs Editor
Kathy Creech

Senior Cartographer
John M. Reijba

Coordinator, Graphics and Design
John Whitney

Production

Director, Manufacturing and Pre-Press
Carma Fazio

Manufacturing Manager
Steven K. Hueppchen

Production/ Technology Manager
Anne Fritzinger

Proofreader
Tina Ramirez

Marketing

Chief Marketing Officer
Patricia Ginnis

Director, Direct Marketing
Mark Willy

Marketing Analyst
Zofia Kulik

For information about other World Book publications, visit our Web site at **http://www.worldbook.com** or call **1-800-WORLDBK (967-5325).** For information about sales to schools and libraries, call **1-800-975-3250 (United States); 1-800-837-5365 (Canada).**

World Book, Inc.
233 N. Michigan Avenue
Chicago, IL 60601
U.S.A.

Printed in the
United States of America

1 2 3 4 5 6 7 8 9 10 09 08 07

Library of Congress Cataloging-in-Publication Data

Insects, spiders, and creepy crawlers: a supplement to Childcraft--
 the how and why library.
  p. cm.
  Summary: "Introduction to insects, spiders, centipedes, and millipedes, including what they are, how they live, and their role in nature, as told through story and illustration. Features include Bug Bytes (fun facts), activity, glossary, resource list, and index" --Provided by publisher.
  Includes bibliographical references and index.
  ISBN 978-0-7166-0618-5
  1. Insects--Juvenile literature.   2. Spiders--Juvenile literature.
I. World Book, Inc. II. Childcraft annual.
QL467.2I67 2007
595.7--dc22

                    2007007033

Contents

Acknowledgments

The publishers of *Childcraft* gratefully acknowledge the courtesy of the following photographers, illustrators, agencies, and organizations for the photographs and illustrations in this volume. When all the illustrations for a sequence of pages are from a single source, the inclusive page numbers are given. Credits should be read from left to right, top to bottom, on the respective pages. All illustrations are the exclusive property of the publisher of *Childcraft* unless names are marked with an asterisk (*).

Covers:
  Aristocrat, Discovery, International and
  Standard Bindings:
    Peter David Scott, The Art Agency
  Heritage Binding:
    © Shutterstock*; Jerry Pinkney;
    © Shutterstock*; Richard Hook;
    © Shutterstock*; © Shutterstock*;
    © Shutterstock*; © Shutterstock*
  Rainbow Binding:
    © Wally Eberhart, Getty Images*

1 WORLD BOOK illustration
2-3 © James P. Blair, Getty Images*
6-7 © Shutterstock*
8-9 © Peter Mason, Getty Images*
10-11 Gwen Connelly
12-13 Hana Sawyer; © Nic Hamilton, Alamy Images*; © Mark Moffett, Minden Pictures*
14-15 © Shutterstock*; Patricia Wynne
16-17 Richard Hook; Hana Sawyer
18-19 © Meul, Nature Picture Library*
20-21 © Luiz Claudio Marigo, Nature Picture Library*; Oxford Scientific Films*
22-23 Richard Hook
24-25 © Grant Heilman*; Gwen Connelly
26-27 © Piotr Naskrecki, Minden Pictures*; © David Scharf, Peter Arnold, Inc.*
28-29 © Edward S. Ross*; © William E. Ferguson*
30-31 Richard Hook
32-33 © Edward S. Ross*; Richard Hook
34-35 © Pete Oxford, Nature Picture Library*
36-37 Gwen Connelly; © Jack Clark, Animals Animals*
38-39 © Edward S. Ross*
40-41 Patricia Wynne; © David Kjaer, Nature Picture Library*
42-45 Wayne Ford, The Art Agency
46-47 © Shutterstock*; © Darlyne A. Murawski, Getty Images*
48-49 © Shutterstock*
50-51 Jerry Pinkney
52-53 Jerry Pinkney; © Shutterstock*
54-55 WORLD BOOK illustrations; © Edward S. Ross*
56-57 © Shutterstock*; © age fotostock/SuperStock*
58-59 © Shutterstock*, Richard Hook; © Kjell B. Sandved*
60-61 WORLD BOOK photo; Richard Hook
62-63 Richard Hook; © Thomas Eisner*
64-65 Richard Hook
66-67 © Edward S. Ross*; WORLD BOOK illustrations
68-69 © Shutterstock*
70-71 Pamela Baldwin Ford
72-73 Pamela Baldwin Ford; © Piotr Naskrecki, Minden Pictures*
74-75 © Stephen Dalton, Photo Researchers*; Jane Burton*
76-77 © Shutterstock*
78-79 © age fotostock/SuperStock*; © Edward S. Ross*
80-81 © SuperStock*
82-83 © Stefano Nicolini, Animals Animals*; © Nancy Rotenberg, Animals Animals*
84-85 © Shutterstock*; © Edward S. Ross*
86-87 Gwen Connelly
88-89 © Edward S. Ross*

90-91 © Edward S. Ross*; Gwen Connelly
92-93 © Edward S. Ross*; © Shutterstock*; © Hulton Archive/Getty Images*
94-95 WORLD BOOK map; © Edward S. Ross*
96-97 Hana Sawyer; Edward S. Ross*
98-99 © Edward S. Ross*; Hana Sawyer; WORLD BOOK illustration; © Kjell B. Sandved*
100-101 © Shutterstock*;
102-103 Jerry Pinkney; © blickwinkel/Alamy Images*
104-109 Jerry Pinkney
110-111 © Edward S. Ross*
112-113 Patricia Wynne
114-115 Jean Helmer
116-117 © Mark Moffett, Minden Pictures*; Norman Weaver
118-119 Jean Helmer
120-121 Patricia Wynne
122-123 © Georgette Douwma, Nature Picture Library*
124-125 © Edward S. Ross*
126-127 © Anthony Bannister, Animals Animals*; © Edward S. Ross*
128-129 © Shutterstock*
130-135 Gwen Connelly
136-137 Gwen Connelly; © Hugh Lansdown, Alamy Images*
138-139 © Shutterstock*; © Scott Camazine, Alamy Images*
140-141 © age fotostock/SuperStock*; © SuperStock*
142-145 Roberta Polfus
146-147 Roberta Polfus; Edward S. Ross*
148-149 © Edward S. Ross*; Susan Stamato
150-151 © Doug Wechsler, Animals Animals*; © Fabio Colobini Medeiros, Animals Animals*
152-153 WORLD BOOK illustration; © Hermann Eisenbeiss, Photo Researchers*
154-155 Patricia Wynne; Edward S. Ross*
156-157 Richard Hook
158-159 Edward S. Ross*; Richard Hook
160-161 Patricia Wynne
162-163 © O.S.F./Animals Animals*; © Shutterstock*
164-167 Roberta Polfus
168-169 © Shutterstock*
170-171 Hana Sawyer
172-173 Patricia Wynne; © Anthony Bannister, Gallo Images/Corbis*
174-175 © Shutterstock*
176-177 © Philip M. DeRenzis, Riser/Getty Images*
178-179 Roberta Polfus; © Hans Pfletschinger, Peter Arnold, Inc.*
180-181 Roberta Polfus; Mark Stowe*; Ann Moreton*
182-183 Jean Helmer
184-185 Roberta Polfus; Oxford Scientific Films*
186-187 Jean Helmer; © Anthony Bannister, Corbis*
188-189 Jack J. Kunz
190-191 WORLD BOOK illustration; © Scott Camazine, Alamy Images*
192-193 WORLD BOOK illustration; © Mary Evans Picture Library/Alamy Images*; Jean Helmer
194-195 Roberta Polfus
196-197 © Shutterstock*
198-199 Jerry Pinkney
200-201 © David M. Dennis, Animals Animals*; WORLD BOOK illustration; AP/Wide World*
202-203 © Edward S. Ross*

Preface

Do you like stories about strange creatures that live on other planets? Many people do.

Most of us like new, astounding, and strange things. Yet, most people don't know that all around them are creatures just as strange, interesting, and exciting as anything there might be on another planet! They are the tiny creatures many of us call "bugs."

You probably don't pay much attention to these tiny creatures. But most of them are actually far more interesting and unusual than many animals you'll see in a zoo! A lot of the tiny creatures are truly as weird as if they came from another planet! Some can do amazing things. And many have astounding ways of life.

These tiny animals also play a big part in our lives—bigger than most of us know. Some destroy our plants, our food and belongings, and even harm us! But some are helpful. And some are very necessary to the world. However, we usually don't know which are which. We often try to kill the very ones we should be glad to see!

This book has two purposes. One is to entertain you with tales as marvelous as any you'll find in fairy tales or science-fiction stories. The other is to open your eyes to the *importance*—for good and bad—of these tiny creatures that we call insects, spiders, and creepy crawlers.

A Kingdom in Your Own Backyard

Animals all around you

Have you ever wanted to watch wild animals up close? Well, you can! And you don't have to go to a zoo, or to Africa, or to the rain forests of South America. Just go to your own backyard, or a place with grass, bushes, trees, and water. Believe it or not, many wild animals live very close to you.

Keep your eyes open. You will find animals that crawl like snakes when they are babies but have wings and fly when they grow up. You'll find fierce hunters that chase their **prey.** You'll see other hunters that lie in wait, make clever traps, or use disguises to get their meals. You'll even find animals that build "cities," have "farms," and keep herds of other animals!

All these creatures are the tiny animals we often call **"bugs."** But it's a mistake to call them all by this name. They are really different kinds of animals—each kind with its own name.

You may not have paid much attention to these tiny animals before. If not, you will be amazed to discover how strange and marvelous they truly are. They are also important. Many of these tiny creatures play a big part in our lives—even though we may not know it.

So turn the page and start to find out about the many kinds of tiny wild animals that are all around you. Learn about their ways of life and the amazing things they do. Then, go out and *see* them do the things you've read about. You'll learn where and how in the activity at the end of this chapter.

The six-legged animals

When the weather is warm, you see many tiny creatures buzzing about in the air, scurrying along the sidewalk, prowling through grass, and creeping over leaves. Most of these little creatures are the animals we call insects.

All insects have six legs. And every insect has a body with three parts—a head, a middle part, and a back part. If you touch an insect, it feels stiff and hard. This is because its body and legs are covered with hard skin. Most insects have feelers on their head. Most insects have wings, but some do not.

There are more than 1 million kinds of insects, and scientists discover thousands of new insects each year. Ants, beetles, bees, butterflies, and grasshoppers are some of the insects you see most often.

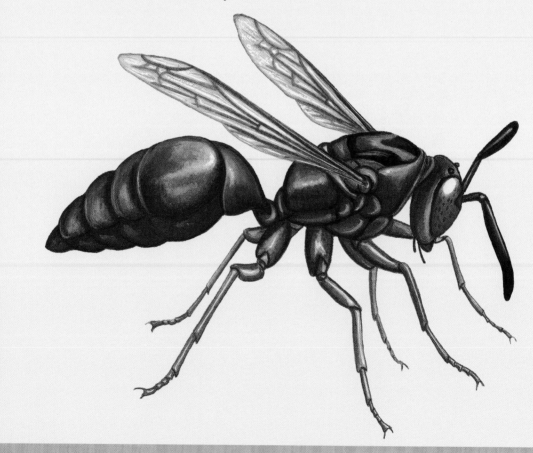

Skipper butterfly

Darkling beetle

Green spider

A Kingdom in Your Own Backyard

The eight-legged animals

Do you think a spider is an insect? It's not!
A spider is a very different kind of animal from
an insect.

Spiders belong to the group of animals called
arachnids *(uh RAK nihdz)*. Arachnids have eight
legs, and insects have only six. The body of an
arachnid is divided into two parts rather than
three like an insect. And no arachnid has wings
or feelers.

Like insects, arachnids have a hard skin.
This hard skin may cover the whole body or only
a part of it. For example, a spider's legs and front
part are covered with an armorlike skin. But its
back part is usually rather soft.

There are more than 50,000 kinds of spiders.
And there are more than 30,000 other kinds of
arachnids. Among the best known of the other
arachnids are scorpions and daddy longlegs.

Lots of legs

Wood lice, also called sow bugs or pill bugs, are not at all like insects or arachnids. These little creatures may have as many as 14 or 16 legs. Like many insects, they have feelers. But they do not have wings.

Wood lice

Although they are called bugs, these tiny animals are actually **crustaceans** (*kruhs TAY shuhnz*). They belong to the same class as shrimps, lobsters, and crabs.

Most crustaceans live in salt water. Like you, they need oxygen to live. You get oxygen out of the air when you breathe. Your lungs take oxygen from the air and pass it into your blood. In this way, the oxygen gets to all parts of your body.

But crustaceans don't have lungs. Instead, they breathe either through their skin or through organs called *gills*. Gills take oxygen from water and pass it into the animal's bloodstream. Wood lice, like most crustaceans, breathe through gills. So, even though they live on land, they have to keep wet in order to breathe.

Wood lice are small, flat, oval-shaped creatures. They look a bit like tiny armadillos. And, like the armadillo, some of them curl themselves into a ball when they are disturbed. A wood louse that does this looks like a small, gray pill. For this reason, it is often called a *pill bug*.

Lots and lots of legs

Have you ever seen animals that look like worms with legs—lots and lots of legs? They may look like worms, but they're not worms. They are animals called centipedes *(SEHN tuh peedz)* and millipedes *(MIHL uh peedz)*.

Centipede means "hundred feet." But some centipedes have only 30 legs. Others have nearly 400. *Millipede* means "thousand feet." But no millipede has this many legs. Some have as few as 24. Others have more than 300 legs—and one species has more than twice that many!

Centipedes and millipedes look alike, but they are really very different. Both have feelers on their head and both have a body that is divided into many sections. But a centipede has two legs—a pair—on each section of its body. A millipede has four legs—two pairs—on each section. The total number of legs each animal has depends on the number of body sections.

Millipede

Plier jaws and sipper tongues

Insects, arachnids, and other many-legged animals don't have the kind of mouth we do. Their mouth is just an open hole.

Insects have special parts around their mouth to help them eat. The kind of mouthparts an insect has depends on the way the insect eats. Some insects, such as ants and dragonflies, chew their food. These insects have two strong jaws that stick out on each side of the mouth. These jaws work like a pair of pliers. With them, the insect tears off pieces of food, such as bits of a leaf.

The inner edges of the jaws are usually lined with little teeth that can grind and cut. The jaws work sideways, not up and down as yours do. If you could hear an insect chewing a bit of leaf, it would sound much like a person chewing celery!

Actually, chewing insects have two sets of jaws. Behind the chewing jaws there is another set of jaws. These jaws are somewhat like fingers. They reach out and take the chewed-up food from the front jaws. Then, the jaws move back and push the food into the animal's mouth.

The little "fingers" near this grasshopper's mouth are its jaws. Many insects have such jaws. They work like a pair of pliers.

This prepona butterfly sips food through a long tube that comes from its mouth. Many insects have such sipping tubes.

Many kinds of insects drink their food. They eat only liquids. So, their mouthparts are made for sucking. A butterfly has a long tube that comes out of its mouth. The tube is coiled up most of the time. But when the butterfly smells nectar, the tube uncoils. Then it is a sipper, like a soda straw.

A mosquito's lower lip contains a long beak with a groove in it. Six sharp "needles" stick out from the end of the beak. The mosquito jabs the needles into the skin of an animal or person, causing blood to flow. Then it sucks up the blood through the groove in its beak. Some kinds of insects suck juice from plants in the same way.

Like all spiders, this jumping
spider has fangs by its mouth.
It kills its prey with the fangs.

A house fly's lower lip forms a tube with a pair of
thick pads on the end. The house fly sops up liquid
with the pads and sucks the liquid up into its mouth.
It can also turn some things, such as sugar, into liquid,
so it can eat them. To do this, it lets "spit" ooze out of
its mouth onto the food. This "spit" turns the solid food
into a liquid.

Spiders turn all of their food into liquid. They first
kill their prey by crushing it or poisoning it. Then, as
the spider sucks the food up through its mouth tube, a
special liquid dissolves it.

Breathing through holes

Inside your chest is a pair of "bags" called lungs. They are much like balloons. When you breathe in, your lungs get larger. This causes them to pull in air. When you breathe out, your lungs get smaller. The air in your lungs is forced out.

An insect doesn't breathe this way. It has no lungs. An insect has a row of little holes on each side of its body. Fresh air seeps into the insect's body through the holes. The air moves about in the insect through a lot of little tubes. The "used-up" air goes back out through the holes in the insect's sides.

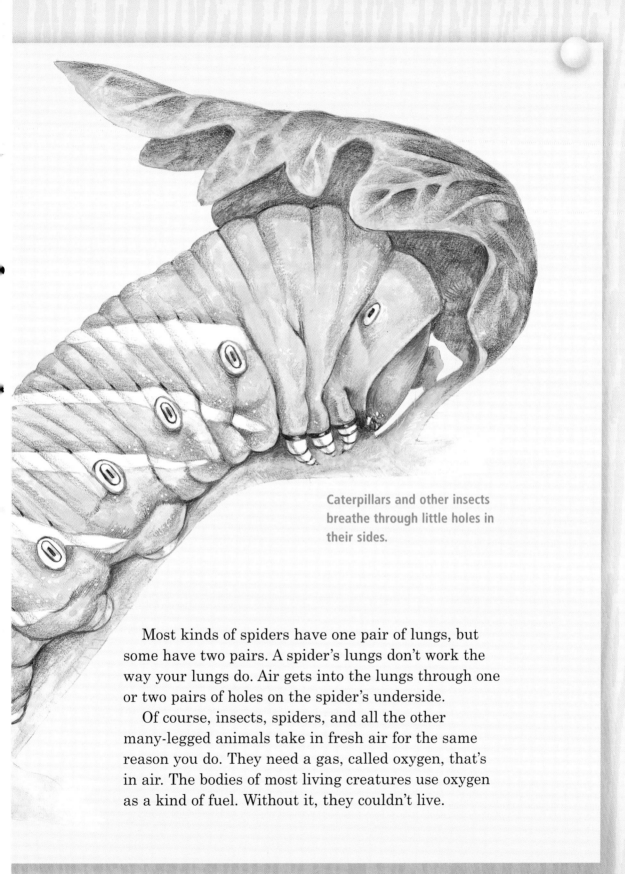

Caterpillars and other insects breathe through little holes in their sides.

Most kinds of spiders have one pair of lungs, but some have two pairs. A spider's lungs don't work the way your lungs do. Air gets into the lungs through one or two pairs of holes on the spider's underside.

Of course, insects, spiders, and all the other many-legged animals take in fresh air for the same reason you do. They need a gas, called oxygen, that's in air. The bodies of most living creatures use oxygen as a kind of fuel. Without it, they couldn't live.

Smelling without a nose

A luna moth skims lightly through the air on pale green wings. It is following a smell that comes from a mile or kilometer away. But the moth isn't sniffing the odor with its nose—it doesn't have a nose. It smells by means of many tiny, hairlike things on its two lacy, feathery feelers, or **antennae.**

Most of the many-legged animals that have feelers use them for smelling. Some kinds of insects also have "smellers" on their mouthparts. And some kinds of insects, as well as spiders, have smellers on their feet. A spider can follow a scent by walking on it!

Luna moth

Tasting with feet

You can't tell if something tastes good by putting your foot on it—but a fly can.

Flies, and several other kinds of insects, taste with their feet! They find good things to eat just by walking around! As a fly walks, it tastes whatever it's walking on. When it steps on something that tastes good, it stops to eat.

Other insects, such as ants and bees, taste with their feelers. When you were on a picnic, did an ant ever touch your sandwich with its feelers? It was probably trying to find out if the sandwich was good to eat.

Insects that chew their food taste with their jaws. They taste their food best when they begin to chew it, just as we do. If something doesn't taste good, the insect stops chewing and gets rid of what it was eating.

"Ears" in strange places

Insects and other many-legged animals have "ears." But their "ears" aren't anything like your ears.

A katydid's "ears" are an opening on each of its front legs. A locust has "ears" on each side of its body. The "ears" of a mosquito are actually tiny hairs on its feelers. And a spider's "ears" are many tiny hairs and slits along its body.

We don't really know if insects and spiders can hear all the things that we can hear. But they can hear the things that are important to them.

A spider can hear a fly that's buzzing in its web. A female katydid can hear the whirring call of a male. And many kinds of moths can hear the high squeaks made by their enemies the bats—a sound we can't hear.

A katydid has an "ear" on each of its front legs. The "ear" is an opening with a piece of thin skin stretched tight behind it.

Seeing with many eyes

Suppose, for a moment, that you could see the world through the eyes of a many-legged animal. What do you think things would look like? Certainly, they would look very different. The eyes of an insect are not like our eyes. And most spiders see things through many eyes! What can that be like?

Most insects have five eyes. Three of the eyes, which are on the insect's forehead, are very tiny and see only light. The other two eyes, which are on each side of the head, are enormous. These are the insect's main eyes.

Each main eye is made up of as few as 6 to as many as 30,000 tiny "eyes." So, instead of seeing one whole, clear "picture" as we do, an insect probably sees things as a great many pieces that fit together to form a single picture. Thus things probably look rather blurry to an insect—like a newspaper picture when you look at it through a magnifying glass.

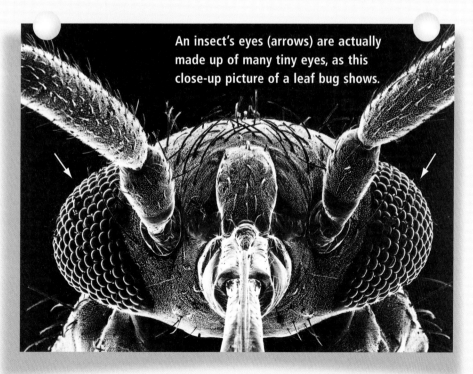

An insect's eyes (arrows) are actually made up of many tiny eyes, as this close-up picture of a leaf bug shows.

Many insects, such as this damselfly, have large, round eyes that let them see in all directions at once.

People see things "whole," like the flower shown left. But insects probably see things in many little pieces, like the flower shown right.

A Kingdom in Your Own Backyard

However, insects can probably see tiny movements better than we can. An insect's big eyes bulge out from its head. Because its eyes stick out, an insect can see ahead, on both sides, and even behind—all at the same time! It easily sees a movement anywhere around it. So it knows when something is trying to creep up on it. And hunting insects are able to find prey more easily.

Insects see some of the colors that we see, but other colors look different to them. A bee sees yellow, blue, violet, and bluish-green. But red looks green to a bee.

However, bees see some colors that we can't see. Scientists have found that some flowers have spots of color that are invisible to us. But bees and some other insects can see these colors.

A spider's eyes, however, aren't like those of an insect. A spider probably sees a whole "picture," just as we do. But most spiders have eight eyes. It is hard to imagine what things look like to a spider!

Some kinds of spiders have six eyes, like this wolf spider. Others have eight eyes.

Feeling with hairs

You feel with your skin. When you touch something, nerves in your skin tell you if the thing is hot, cold, wet, dry, smooth, rough, soft, hard, slick, or sticky.

An insect can't feel anything with its hard, armorlike skin. But insects have many tiny hairs growing out through their armor. They use these hairs to feel all the things we can feel. Spiders and other many-legged creatures also have such hairs on their body.

Insects have a great many of these "touch hairs" on their feelers. As an insect walks about, it "explores" everything with its feelers, touching them to everything it comes into contact with. With their feelers, many insects can tell how a thing feels, smells, and tastes—all at the same time!

Insects use their antennae to touch and feel. Tiny hairs on the antennae of these blister beetles tell them what things feel like.

So, an insect's feelers are very important. Often, you'll see an insect bend its head and rub its feelers with its front legs. It does this to clean its feelers. It cleans them by pulling them through a special sort of "comb" on its leg. This helps keep the feelers in good working order.

Some insects can feel things we can't feel. Did you ever try to smack a fly with your hand? The fly nearly always zooms away before you can hit it. The hairs on the fly's body can feel the air moving as your hand comes down. This warns the fly to take off at once.

Noisemakers

Many insects are noisy! A fly can fill a whole room with a loud buzz as it soars and circles about. On a warm summer night, insects often keep up a steady chirp, creak, and whir. Do the noises *mean* anything? And how do the insects make these noises?

Some of the noises that insects make are not made on purpose. They just happen. The buzzing or humming sound that a flying insect makes is the sound of its wings moving very rapidly. For most insects, the sound doesn't mean anything. But for some insects, the sounds they make are important.

The African insect called a bulla makes "music" by scraping its legs against a row of bumps on its sides.

The sound made by a female mosquito's wings help a male mosquito find her. A male can tell the sound of a female's wings even though there may be other noises around. By flying toward the sound, the male finds a mate.

Many of the chirps, creaks, and whirs of insects, however, are made on purpose. The insects make the noises by rubbing special parts of their bodies together, or by making a special part vibrate, or shake, rapidly.

Most of the sounds are made by male insects. They make use of some sounds to call females to them. A female goes toward the sound and finds the male. They mate, and in time she will lay eggs.

But some sounds mean other things. Some male crickets have special "territories" that they "own." If another male cricket comes into the territory, the "owner" makes a special noise that's a warning. It means, "Get out or I'll fight you!"

Often, a whole group of the same kind of insect will make the same kind of noise. This is a way of calling others of their kind, both males and females, to come to them. A grasshopper that's alone will head toward noise made by a group of others of its kind. This brings many grasshoppers together so they can find mates easily.

Insects aren't the only many-legged animals that make noise. Some kinds of male spiders also have special body parts they rub together to make noise.

Growing up

Suppose you saw two flies standing close together. And suppose one fly was much smaller than the other. You would probably think the small one was a baby fly.

Actually, they would be two different kinds of flies. And both would be grown-ups. You can always tell a grown-up insect by its wings. Baby insects don't have wings. Baby insects aren't little creatures that look like their parents, as do many kinds of baby animals. Most baby insects don't look at all like their parents.

A fly begins life inside an egg. The egg looks like a grain of rice. When the egg hatches, usually in a few hours, out comes the baby fly.

The baby fly doesn't look a bit like a grown-up fly. It has no wings, no feelers, and no legs. It looks like a tiny white worm. Many kinds of baby insects look like worms. Such wormlike babies are called **larvae** *(LAHR vee)*.

Larvae don't do anything but eat and grow. But their skins don't grow, as ours do. A larva *(LAHR vuh)* grows *inside* its skin. When the skin becomes too tight, it splits open, usually down the back. Then the larva crawls out of the old skin! It may do this several times while it is "growing up."

A time comes when the larva has eaten enough and grown enough. Then it spins a silk covering, or forms a sort of shell around itself. Now it has become what is called a **pupa** *(PYOO puh)*.

The young insect lies quietly inside its covering. Slowly, its body changes. It grows long legs and feelers. In most cases it grows wings—although some kinds of grown-up insects don't have wings. After some time it breaks out of its covering. Now it has a body exactly like that of its parents. It has grown up. It will never grow any bigger.

A young katydid is pulling itself out of its old skin. All young insects grow by shedding their hard outer skin from time to time.

Adult

Egg

Larva
(Caterpillar)

Pupa
(Chrysalis)

A butterfly, like many other insects, has four
stages of life. It begins life as a tiny egg.
When it breaks out of the shell it is a wormlike
larva, or caterpillar. The caterpillar becomes
a pupa. A hard shell, called a chrysalis, forms
around the pupa. Inside the shell, the pupa
changes into an adult butterfly.

Some kinds of insect babies, such as grasshoppers, are only a little different from their parents. They have legs and feelers. But they may have shorter, stubby bodies. And, at this age, they don't yet have wings. This kind of insect baby is called a **nymph** *(nihmf)*.

A nymph is tiny when it comes out of its egg. It, too, grows by climbing out of its skin from time to time. Each time, its body gets a little bigger and its wings grow a bit. Finally, its wings swell up to full size. Now the insect is an adult. It will never grow any more.

Some kinds of wingless insects, as well as spiders, centipedes, and millipedes, have babies that look just like their parents. These babies, too, often **molt,** or shed their skin and grow a new one. Some kinds keep on growing all their lives. Even after they are adults, they shed their skin and get bigger from time to time.

Aphids, like some other kinds of insects, have babies that look exactly like their parents. The larger aphids are adults.

Can they think?

When an insect comes out of its egg it is ready for life. It knows what kind of food to eat and how to get it. It knows what certain sounds and smells mean. It doesn't have to learn any of these things. And it doesn't think about them. It is simply able to do them.

An insect's body contains many "messages." As the creature moves about, "messages" tell it what to do next. A certain smell may give it a message to taste. A certain taste will give it a message to eat. And so on. Most of the things an insect does are done because of these messages—not because the insect thought about doing them.

Some insects can learn things. A bee can be taught to go to a certain color for food. And some insects can remember things. A hunter wasp seems to find its way back to its nest by remembering landmarks. So insects have a kind of intelligence. But none of them can think as a human does—or even as well as a dog or cat does.

A honey bee can be taught to go to a color for food, such as this gold on a sunflower.

Are they important?

Insects are *very* important. The world could get along without people—but it *couldn't* get along without insects!

For one thing, insects and other many-legged creatures are important food for many kinds of fish, birds, and other animals. If all the insects were to suddenly vanish, all the creatures that eat them would soon die.

Insects are just as important to many plants. All flowers become some kind of fruit or vegetable with seeds in it. But to make this happen, some flowers need pollen from another flower of its kind. Insects, such as butterflies and bees, play a big role in carrying pollen from one flower to another.

Thus, without insects, there wouldn't be many kinds of fruits and vegetables—such as apples, cherries, oranges, grapes, pears, carrots, cabbages, and onions! And, of course, all these kinds of plants would soon disappear, because there wouldn't be any seeds from which new plants could grow.

Many insects that live in the soil help keep the soil fertile so that plants can grow in it. And many kinds of insects and many-legged animals do important work as nature's garbage collectors. They feed on the remains of dead animals and plants.

Several kinds of insects provide people with useful things. Honey, which is a very good food, is made by bees. Bees also make a wax that people use to make candles, shoe polish, furniture polish, and other things. Silk cloth is made from threads spun by certain kinds of caterpillars. Several kinds of medicine also come from parts of insects' bodies.

We think of all these useful insects as helpful insects. But there are other kinds of insects that we think of as harmful.

Many kinds of insects damage plants and trees by eating parts of them or laying eggs in them. Such insects are a terrible problem to farmers. They destroy food that people need. They also kill such useful plants as cotton. There are also insects that do great damage to wood, to cloth, and to stored foods such as flour, cheese, and meat.

Even worse, some insects are a danger to people because they carry germs that cause diseases. The disease called malaria *(muh LAIR ee uh)* kills at least a million people each year. Malaria is carried by a certain kind of mosquito. A certain kind of fly carries the disease called sleeping sickness. This disease is a serious problem in Africa. Even ordinary house flies can carry diseases, as can ticks, lice, and fleas.

Many insects are harmful to plant life. The larvae of bark beetles kill trees, such as redwoods, by digging tunnels in the trunk and branches.

Tunnels made by bark beetle larvae

Insects are, indeed, important. Some are important because they cause us serious trouble. Others are important because they are useful to us. But we shouldn't think of insects and other many-legged animals as "good" or "bad." Like all wild creatures, they are simply doing what they must to stay alive. They are part of the great web of life that includes every living plant and animal.

Insects are an important part of the great web of life that includes all plants and animals. As this hawk moth feeds on a thistle, it helps to spread the flower's pollen, assuring the plant's survival.

Looking for Insects, Spiders, and Creepy Crawlers

You will need:

Magnifying glass

Flashlight

Rubber or
  plastic gloves

Sharp knife [Caution: have
  an adult handle the knife]

Pen or pencil

Paper

Insects, spiders, and other creepy crawlers are all around you! You can learn about them by exploring different habitats. A habitat is the environment or area that is the natural home of certain plants and animals.

Look closely at small habitats such as a bush, a tree, a pond, a compost heap, or even a window box, to see what kind of tiny creatures live there.

It is always safest to observe only, rather than to touch or handle insects, spiders, and other small creatures. **Be sure to wear gloves to protect your hands** as you explore these different environments.

Life on leaves and stems

Garden plants often show signs of insect activity. Look in a garden to see what you can find on the leaves and stems of plants.

Leafcutting bee

• Look carefully on a blackberry bush and you may find that some of the leaves are rolled up. Can you see a caterpillar inside?

- Little white lines on a blackberry leaf may have been caused by insects called leafminer flies. Hold a leaf up to the light, or hold a flashlight behind it to see if you can detect the insects tunneling through the leaf.

- If you look closely at the leaves on a rosebush you will probably find that some have been nibbled around the edges. This is a sign that a leafcutting bee has been taking away pieces of leaf to make cocoons for its eggs.

- If the stems and buds of roses are sticky and green, this is probably a mass of aphids which suck the sap inside the plant. You may also see a ladybug feeding on the aphids.

- Froth on the stem of a plant is evidence of a froghopper, which lives inside the bubbles that are known as "cuckoo spit." See if you can find some in your yard or a park.

- Swellings on grass stems or leaves may contain the larvae of flies or moths. They are called *galls*. Take some home and **ask an adult to open them carefully with a sharp knife.** Sometimes they contain a spider, ant, or thrip that has moved into the empty gall.

Ladybug

Aphids

Gall

Making a "room" out of a mushroom

Fungi, such as mushrooms, provide homes and food for many insects. If you look at the gills under the cap of a fully grown wild mushroom or toadstool, you may see little black specks. Look with a magnifying glass and you will see that each speck is the head of a little larva. Break open the cap to see how the larvae eat tiny tunnels through it. **Always wash your hands after touching fungi; never eat wild fungi.**

Tree of life

A tree, such as an oak, is a habitat for thousands of creatures. The leaves, fruits, and seeds are food for beetles, ants, aphids, bees, wasps, moths, and many more insects, which in turn are eaten by birds and mammals. Count how many kinds of insects you see buzzing around or crawling on a single tree. You may be surprised to discover that the tree is alive with wildlife. Make a note of the insects that you see and what they are doing.

Insect larvae

Deathwatch beetle larva

A "log cabin" for tiny creatures

All kinds of creatures burrow into rotting wood and tree bark. If you find a fallen tree or tree limb, look in the bark litter near the tree for insects living there.

1. Peel away a little moss or bark to see what is living beneath it. You may find beetles, earwigs, or even a centipede. Centipedes often hunt small insects.

2. Break off part of the log to see if there are burrowing insects. Holes and tunnels in the wood may be caused by burrowing deathwatch beetle larvae. **Wash your hands after touching tree litter.**

Wasp nest

Beetles

Wasp

Centipede

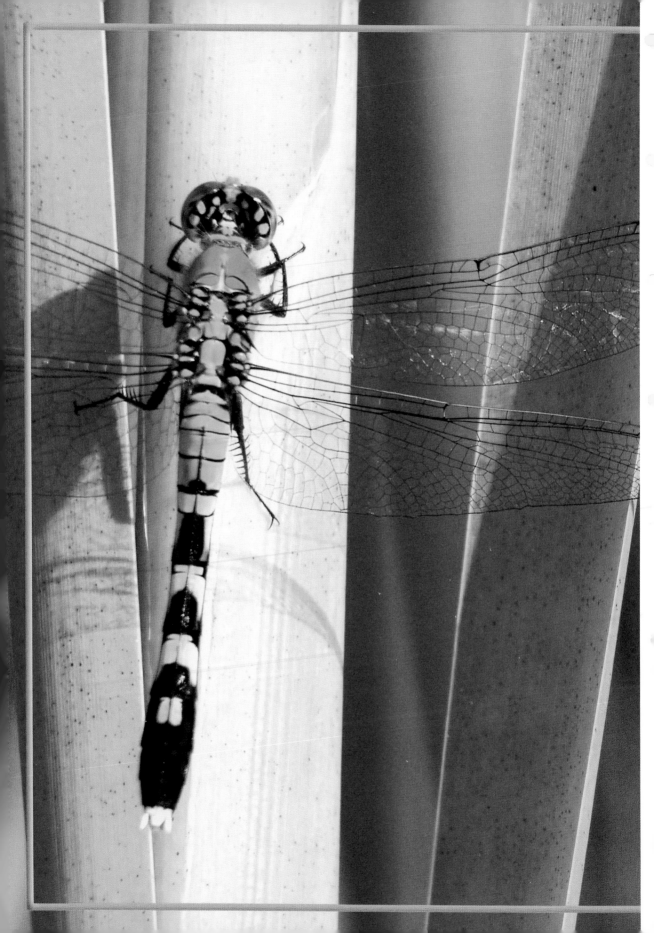

Dragons and Damsels

Dragonfly fables

Have you ever seen a "darning needle," or a "horse stinger," or a "mosquito hawk"? You have if you've seen a dragonfly. These are all nicknames for the dragonfly.

Dragonflies have a lot of nicknames. They're often called *darning needles,* or *devil's darning needles.* People once believed that a dragonfly could use its thin, needle-like body to sew up a person's ears, eyes, and mouth!

Dragonflies have also been called *horse stingers,* because they often hover around horses and appear to be stinging them. But the real stingers are the flies the dragonflies are trying to catch! Dragonflies do *not* sting. You can hold a dragonfly in your hand or let it cling to your finger. It won't bite you—and it can't sting you.

But dragonflies do attack other insects. They're fierce, swift hunters. They've earned the name *mosquito hawks* because of the way they dart after mosquitoes, seizing them in midair. Dragonflies are also called *bee hawks* and *bee butchers,* because they kill and eat many honey bees.

Folk tales from the southern United States claim that dragonflies take care of snakes, so many people there call them *snake doctors.* This is because they think that dragonflies "look after" snakes! Some people even believe that a "snake doctor" can bring a dead snake back to life!

Dragonfly

The two lives of a dragonfly

The green stems of plants poke up from the water of the little pond. Inside the stem of one plant, just under the surface of the water, lies a tiny egg. The egg has been in the plant stem for about 10 days.

Suddenly, the egg begins to quiver. The little creature inside is breaking out. Using three sharp points on its tail, the creature makes an opening in the egg. Then it pushes its way out and onto the stem of the plant.

The newborn animal has a jointed, greenish-brown body and six legs. Two big, bulgy, yellowish eyes on its large head stare out at the watery world of the pond. It is a baby dragonfly—about to begin the first of its two lives.

The dragonfly baby, or **nymph,** is all ready for life in the pond, even though it has only just hatched. It breathes through gills in the end of its body. It swims by sucking water into its gills, then quickly squirting it out. This makes the nymph shoot forward, just as a balloon does when you let the air squirt out of it.

The nymph knows exactly how to get its food. Clinging to the stem of the plant, it waits. After a time, another creature comes wriggling up through the water. It has a long, jointed body, but is much smaller than the nymph. It is a mosquito baby, or **larva.**

The nymph waits, silent and motionless. The mosquito larva comes nearer and nearer. Suddenly, part of the nymph's head seems to shoot out toward the larva! It is like a broad, flat arm with two claws. Actually, this is one of the nymph's mouth parts—the lower lip. Most of the time this lower lip is folded flat on the underside of the nymph's head.

The two claws seize the larva, digging into its soft body. Then the lip folds back, carrying the larva to the nymph's mouth. While the claws hold the larva fast, the nymph begins to chew the helpless larva and stuff the pieces into its mouth!

This is how the nymph spends most of its time. Clinging to a plant stem, it lies in wait for smaller creatures to come along. If the hunting isn't good in one place, it swims to another place.

The nymph is a dreadful danger to the tiny creatures of the pond. But it is also always in danger. There are many larger hunters in the pond, such as giant water bugs and frogs. Many of the nymph's brothers and sisters are eaten by these creatures. Life in the pond is one of constant danger. It is a struggle to stay alive.

From time to time, the nymph takes off its skin. The skin becomes brittle and splits across the back. With a lot of pushing and wiggling, the nymph pulls itself free. The old skin is left behind, like a pale, hollow statue of the nymph.

Each time the nymph sheds its skin, the nymph is a little bigger. After it has shed its skin several times, little stubby wings appear on its back.

The nymph stays in the pond for about two years. Then, a special day arrives. The nymph is ready to shed its skin for the last time.

The nymph crawls up a plant stem until it is above the water. There it rests in the warm summer sunshine, its six legs gripping the plant stem. Slowly it begins to push its way out of the split in its old skin. Bit by bit, it jerks and wiggles itself free. Then it rests, sitting on top of its old skin, which is as transparent as glass.

During the next half hour, the nymph slowly grows and changes. Its stubby wings swell until they are long and lacy. The nymph has become a dragonfly—and started the second of its two lives. This second life will last from only a few weeks to several months.

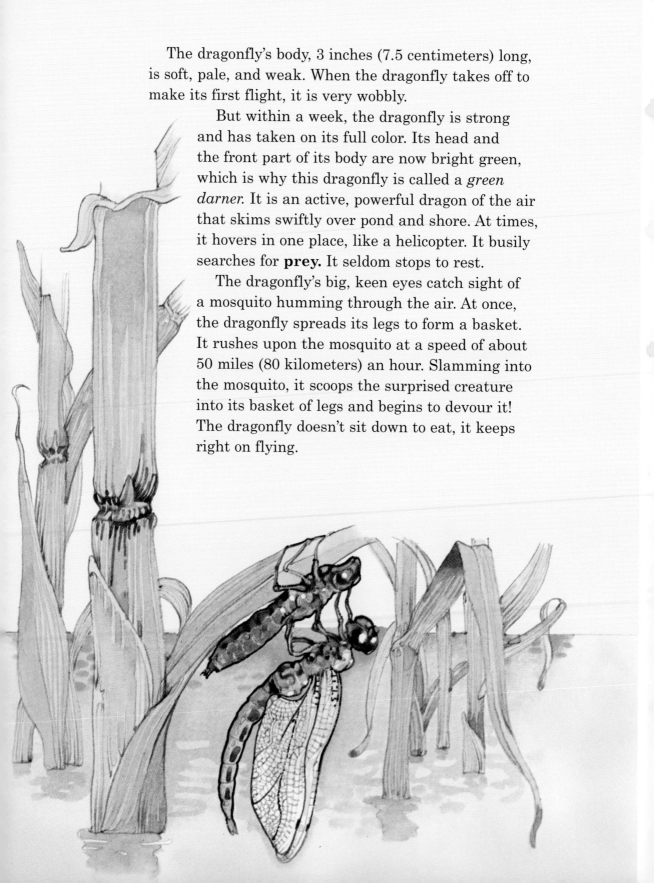

The dragonfly's body, 3 inches (7.5 centimeters) long, is soft, pale, and weak. When the dragonfly takes off to make its first flight, it is very wobbly.

But within a week, the dragonfly is strong and has taken on its full color. Its head and the front part of its body are now bright green, which is why this dragonfly is called a *green darner.* It is an active, powerful dragon of the air that skims swiftly over pond and shore. At times, it hovers in one place, like a helicopter. It busily searches for **prey.** It seldom stops to rest.

The dragonfly's big, keen eyes catch sight of a mosquito humming through the air. At once, the dragonfly spreads its legs to form a basket. It rushes upon the mosquito at a speed of about 50 miles (80 kilometers) an hour. Slamming into the mosquito, it scoops the surprised creature into its basket of legs and begins to devour it! The dragonfly doesn't sit down to eat, it keeps right on flying.

Young dragonfly

The dragonfly now has a different kind of mouth than it had when it was a nymph. Its lower lip is shaped like a bowl, with hooks around the edge. The dragonfly uses this lip like a plate. The hooks hold the mosquito while the dragonfly chews it to pieces.

The dragonfly is now a terror of the air, just as it was a terror of the pond when it was a nymph. But, just as it was always in danger as a nymph, it is also in danger as a dragonfly. At any moment, it may be snatched out of the air by a hungry bird. And, if it stops to rest on a leaf or plant stem, a bullfrog may gobble it up.

For several weeks, the female dragonfly spends the warm summer days flying about. At times she alights on a plant stem and clings there to rest. But she cannot walk.

Finally, the time comes when the dragonfly is ready to mate. There are eggs in her body. As she flies, a male dragonfly comes to join her. Still flying, the two of them cling together and mate in the air.

Then, still clinging together, the two tiny, gleaming dragons sail down toward the surface of the pond. They hover beside the stem of a plant growing up out of the water. The female dips the end of her long body into the water and pushes it into the stem of the plant. She lays one of her eggs inside the plant. There, it will be safe and protected. Soon, a little nymph will hatch—ready to begin the first of its two lives.

Bug Bytes

How do you tell a damselfly from a dragonfly?

Damselflies and dragonflies look much alike. But when a damselfly rests, it holds its wings together (above left). A resting dragonfly holds its wings straight out (above right). Dragonflies are also stronger fliers and they usually have joined eyes, unlike damselflies.

Damselflies

Damselflies are cousins of dragonflies. The word *damsel* means "a young girl," and damselflies are smaller and slimmer than dragonflies.

A damselfly nymph has three feathery, tail-like gills which allow it to breath underwater. It moves through the water by wriggling from side to side.

Like dragonflies, damselflies are fierce hunters and skim close to the water of streams and ponds in search of prey. Their way of life is much like that of dragonflies.

A damselfly is smaller and more slender than a dragonfly.

Meet the Beetles

The plant protectors

The plant leaf is covered with tiny green insects. These insects, called aphids *(AY fihdz),* suck juices out of plants. In time, they will kill this plant!

But, suddenly, a flying creature alights on the leaf and folds its wings with a click. It is a round-bodied, red-and-black ladybug.

The ladybug is quite a bit bigger than the aphids. Marching to the nearest aphid, the ladybug seizes it and gobbles it down! One after another, the ladybug eats the aphids until all are gone!

Ladybugs are very useful. They eat aphids and other insects that destroy many kinds of plants we use for food. In the late 1800's, a type of scale insect threatened to destroy the fruit crop in California. But the fruit was saved by turning thousands of ladybugs loose.

There are more than 5,000 different kinds of lady-bugs in the world. Many are red or yellow with black spots. Some are black with red or yellow spots. Their bright colors are probably a "warning" to birds that ladybugs taste bad. And, birds usually leave them alone.

The bright-colored back of a ladybug is really two hard wing covers. If you watch a ladybug getting ready to fly, you'll see its colored back split in two as it lifts its wing covers out of the way of its wings. Most kinds of beetles have wing covers. Wing covers are one of the things that make them beetles.

Ladybug and aphids

Tiger beetles

Many of the beetles you see scuttling about on a warm, sunny day are probably tiger beetles. They're called tigers because they hunt like tigers. They creep up on a smaller insect, then rush at it, seize it, and munch it down!

A mother tiger beetle digs tunnels and lays one egg in each. The **larvae** (babies) that hatch out look like long-legged caterpillars. Like their parents, they're meat-eaters. But they have a different way of hunting. After a larva hatches, it lies in wait just inside the entrance to its tunnel. When an insect passes close by, the larva rears out and grabs it. Then the larva pulls its captive into the tunnel and eats it!

There are many kinds of tiger beetles. Most of them are brightly colored and shiny. You can find some kinds on sandy beaches, some in woods, and some in gardens—where they help to keep out harmful pests.

A tiger beetle larva (above right) looks like a long-legged caterpillar. Six-spotted green tiger beetles (above left), like many adult tiger beetles, are brightly colored and shiny.

59

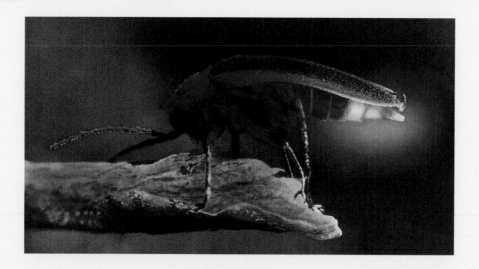

Flying flashlights

It is a summer evening, just at twilight. Long shadows fall across the grassy meadow and filter through the nearby forest. Suddenly, scores of tiny, flashing lights drift through the gathering darkness. The fireflies have come out.

Fireflies, also known as *lightning bugs,* are neither flies nor bugs. They are really beetles. You can often see them during the day, crawling or resting on leaves. At twilight, the males begin to fly and flash their lights. The females flash their lights in answer. The flashing lights are a signal that helps male and female fireflies find each other so they can mate.

A firefly's light comes from the underside of the firefly's body, near the back end. A firefly has special chemicals in its body. When these chemicals mix with oxygen, a gas that is in the air, the firefly is able to make a light. This light is a cold light—there is almost no heat. It is not like the lights we know how to make, which give off heat as well as light.

Firefly larvae hatch from eggs. These babies, which look somewhat like caterpillars, are fierce hunters! At night, they creep beneath loose earth and dead leaves in search of snails, worms, and the larvae of other insects. A firefly larva shoots poison into its prey with its mouthparts. The poison turns the creature's insides to liquid, which the larva then sucks out.

A few kinds of adult fireflies are also hunters. But many kinds don't eat at all. They live only to mate. Then they die.

Some kinds of female fireflies don't have wings. They look much like caterpillars. In some places, these wingless fireflies are called *glowworms*.

A firefly flashes its light on and off as a mating signal.

A beetle with a "cannon"!

Squatting in a woods, a frog watches a dark, shiny beetle with a red head. When the beetle is close enough, the frog jumps at it. The frog's sticky tongue shoots out. The beetle sticks to it and is pulled into the frog's mouth.

But, as the frog's tongue touches the beetle, there is a muffled *pop!* It sounds like a tiny cannon being fired. Instantly, the frog spits out the beetle and begins to choke and gag. The beetle scurries away.

The unlucky frog has tried to eat a bombardier *(bahm buh DEER)* beetle. But this kind of beetle is well able to defend itself. The word *bombardier* originally meant "one who fires a cannon."

A bombardier beetle (below and in photo, right) defends itself by squirting a hot, irritating jet of gas at its attacker.

And the bombardier beetle has a sort of cannon in its back end! It can shoot out a burning, stinging cloud of liquid. Any bird, reptile, or other creature that gets a blast from the beetle's cannon in its mouth will drop the beetle at once!

Bombardier beetles are quite common in many parts of the United States and Canada. A bombardier beetle that is black with four yellow spots is common in Australia.

Bombardier beetles are about half an inch (12.7 millimeters) long. These insects are useful because they eat many kinds of harmful insects.

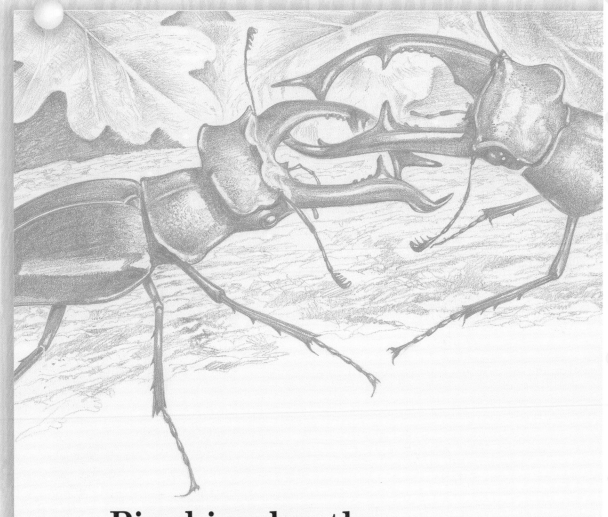

Pinching beetles

Two large brown beetles face each other on a log.
They have their big, curved jaws, nearly as long as
their entire bodies, wide open.

Suddenly, one beetle charges! The beetles bump
together, struggling and pushing and clicking their
jaws. Finally, one beetle tumbles backward and slips
off the log. The fight is over. Nearby, a female beetle
waits. The fight was over her! She would now be the
winner's mate.

These big-jawed beetles are called *stag beetles*.
This is because their jaws look like the antlers of a

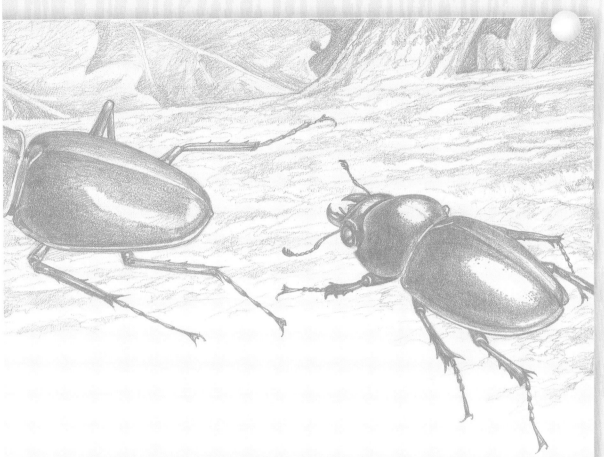

stag, or male deer. Only the males have these big jaws. Scientists aren't sure why because the jaws aren't good for much. They are so big and awkward that they often seem to get in the way. But they don't prevent the beetles from flying.

One kind of stag beetle is called a *pinchingbug* because the jaws look as if they ought to be able to give a good pinch. Actually, the big jaws of the males are quite weak. But the females, which have much smaller jaws, can really give you a pinch—one that will make your finger bleed!

Stag beetles look fierce, but they aren't. They feed mostly on sap that oozes out of trees. Stag beetle larvae look like fat white worms. The larvae eat the rotting wood of old logs and stumps, where the mother beetles lay their eggs.

Weevils

If you ever happen to see a beetle that looks as if it has a very long nose, it is probably a *weevil*. Because of their long "noses," weevils are also known as *snout beetles*.

The snout isn't a nose. It is actually a long mouth with jaws at the end. Having such a long mouth enables a snout beetle to chew deep into things. Mother snout beetles chew deep tunnels into nuts, fruits, seeds, and the stems and roots of plants. Then they lay eggs in the tunnels. When the larvae hatch, they have all the food they need.

The weevil family is the biggest of all the animal families in the world! There are at least 40,000 different kinds of these creatures. That's more than all the different kinds of birds, reptiles (snakes and lizards), amphibians (frogs and toads), and mammals (furry, milk-bearing animals) put together!

Many kinds of weevils are pests. They spoil many kinds of fruits, nuts, seeds, grain, and vegetables. Some kill trees. One kind, called a *boll weevil,* does terrible damage to cotton plants.

But some weevils are a help to us. We use them to kill plants that are growing where they aren't wanted.

Both beetles are life-size!

Bug Bytes

Super beetles!

The Goliath beetle (top) lives in Africa. It can grow up to 5 inches (13 centimeters) long and is the heaviest of all insects. It eats mostly nectar and pollen.

The eastern Hercules beetle (above right) is one of the largest beetles in North America. It grows to 2½ inches (6 centimeters) long. The male uses its long horn in a "duel" with another male. The female has a very small horn or none at all.

Grasshoppers and Their Relatives

The life of a grasshopper

It is September in the Midwest. The air is warm and sunny. The trees are green and shaggy with leaves. In a golden, grassy meadow, a mother grasshopper is ready to lay her eggs.

At the end of her long body are several hard, sharp points. She pushes these into the ground, drilling a deep hole into the soft dirt. Then, from the end of her tail, she drops a number of tiny eggs into the hole.

A foamy, sticky stuff comes out of the grasshopper's body along with the eggs. This sticky stuff quickly dries, covering all the eggs. It is like a sponge, full of holes through which air can reach the eggs.

Now, with a great leap, the grasshopper soars away. She will dig several more holes and lay more clumps of eggs. Each clump may hold from 20 to 70 eggs. At this time of year, a great many mother grasshoppers are laying eggs, so there are thousands of eggs buried in the meadow.

Many of these eggs will never hatch. The meadow is filled with the **larvae** of blister beetles and several kinds of flies—creatures that eat grasshopper eggs.

Autumn comes to the meadow. The leaves change color and drop from the trees. The green, juicy plants of summer turn to dry, withered husks. The adult grasshoppers are all dead. After a time, snow falls. The ground freezes.

The cold of winter actually makes the tiny creatures inside the eggs begin to grow. This is nature's way of helping them. If the eggs simply needed warmth to hatch, they might hatch too soon. Then the baby grasshoppers would be caught without food at the beginning of winter.

Winter comes to an end. The spring sun warms the meadow. New green plants begin to push up out of the earth. Inside their eggs, the baby grasshoppers begin to stir. They are ready to come out into a world that will be warm and full of food.

One of the eggs splits at the top. The baby grasshopper pushes its way out. It is wrapped in a sort of loose skin that holds the grasshopper's legs against its body. The grasshopper crawls upward, like a worm, through the tunnels and holes of the material that forms the clump of eggs. It pushes its way through the dirt. Finally, it breaks out into the air and light.

The crawling and pushing causes the wrapper of loose skin to split. The skin shrinks and slides off. Now the baby can stand up on its six legs. Unlike many baby insects, it looks like its parents, except that it has no wings.

As if to celebrate its new life, the little creature makes a mighty 4-inch (10-centimeter) jump. This would be about 120 feet (37 meters) for a tall person!

The young grasshopper's main interest is food. Different kinds of grasshoppers eat different things. Many kinds eat grass. But some eat garden plants and farm crops.

The young grasshopper eats and grows. It has to crawl out of its outer skin about six times during the first six weeks of its life. Each time, its body is longer and its wings have grown a bit. The last time, its wings swell up and become full size. The grasshopper is now full grown. It may be 1 to 3 or more inches (2.5 to 7.6 centimeters) long, depending on the kind of grasshopper it is.

Almost every minute of its life, the grasshopper is in danger. A bird may swoop down on it, or it may be seized by another insect. Frogs, toads, and snakes may gobble it up. So may raccoons and skunks. And some kinds of wasps hunt female grasshoppers. They carry them off to be food for baby wasps.

The grasshopper's best defense is to jump away. It does this with its wings spread, to carry it in a great, curving glide. Its greenish or brownish color also helps it to hide in grass or among leaves.

Throughout the long, warm days of summer, the grasshopper walks, hops, and glides about in the meadow. Because it eats grass, it has plenty of food.

This grasshopper is a male, so it can make "music." As it flies, it makes a crackling sound. It does this by rubbing its front wings and back legs together. On each back leg there is a "scraper." This is like a tiny comb with many teeth. And each wing has a thick ridge. The grasshopper makes its "song" by rubbing the scrapers against the ridges. Near the end of summer, a female grasshopper is attracted to

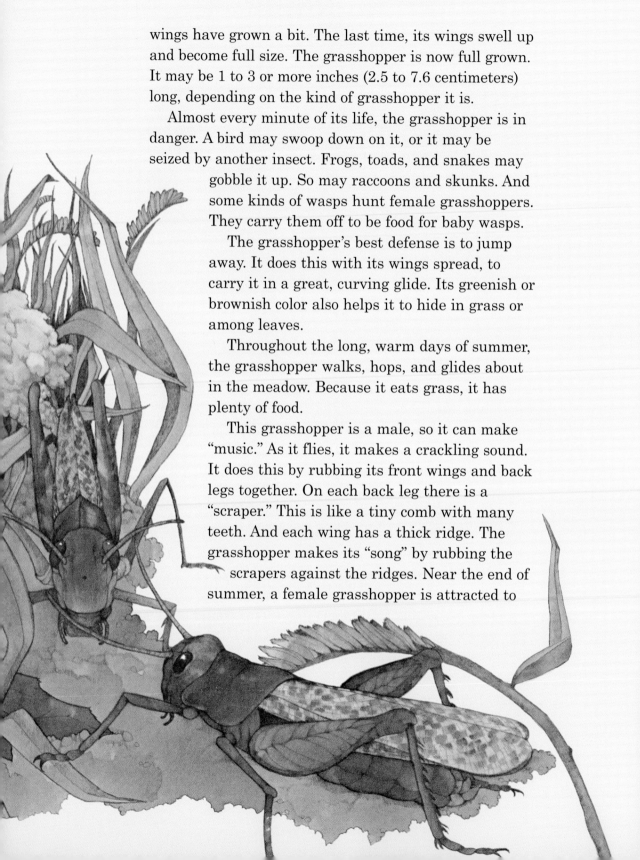

the male's song. She comes to where he is. They stand facing each other, their **antennae** (feelers) touching. It is almost as if they are getting acquainted. They meet this way for several days. Finally, one day, they mate. Soon, the female will lay her eggs.

The male grasshopper keeps making his music for a time. But as the days pass, he makes it less and less often. And it becomes softer and softer. After about a week, it stops.

The grasshopper no longer eats. Soon, he stops moving. His short summer of life in the sunny meadow has come to an end.

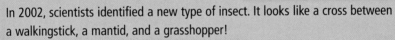

Bug Bytes

A whole new type of insect

In 2002, scientists identified a new type of insect. It looks like a cross between a walkingstick, a mantid, and a grasshopper!

The insect lives in southern Africa. It grows from ½ to 1½ inches (1 to 4 centimeters) long. It is different from a walkingstick in that its first body segment is the largest. Unlike a mantid, it uses its middle legs as well as its front legs to catch prey. And unlike a grasshopper, it cannot jump.

The insect always holds the last segment of each leg in the air, even when walking. This makes the insect look like it is walking on its "heels." So scientists named this group of insects *heelwalkers*. Some scientists also nicknamed the new animal "the gladiator" for its fearsome appearance and the "armor" that covers it as a nymph.

Scientists discover thousands of new species of insects every year, but this was the first time in 87 years that researchers identified a whole new order (group) of insects!

Grasshopper trouble!

Grasshoppers often cause trouble—terrible trouble! Sometimes enormous numbers of grasshoppers hatch at about the same time. They begin to move across the land, eating as they go. Soon, they are able to fly. When they all take off in a gigantic swarm, billions of grasshoppers darken the sky!

Where one of these swarms comes down, there is dreadful destruction! The billions of grasshoppers eat every green plant and leaf in their path. They can destroy hundreds of square miles or square kilometers of farm crops. If they come to a town, they often fill the streets in such numbers that people can't walk or drive. Parts of rivers may even become filled up with the bodies of dead grasshoppers.

The grasshoppers that cause all of this trouble and damage are called **locusts.** They are among the kinds of grasshopper known as short-horned grasshoppers because they have short feelers, or "horns." No one knows why so many of them sometimes appear so suddenly.

Locust

Katydid-katydid

On late summer and autumn nights, the air may be filled with a noise that, to some people, sounds like "katydid-katydid." This sound is made by the kind of grasshopper called a *katydid*. Katydids are a type of long-horned grasshopper, because they have long feelers, or "horns."

Although you can hear katydids, you seldom see them. That's because they're usually high in the trees. Their wings look like leaves, and their bodies are green, so they blend right in.

Long-horned grasshoppers don't make their "music" the way short-horned grasshoppers do. Instead of rubbing their back legs against their front wings, they rub a sharp edge on one front wing against a row of bumps on the other front wing. Usually only the males make a noise. They do this to attract females.

Katydid

A "praying" hunter

A large green insect stands in a clump of grass. It blends into the grass so well it can hardly be seen. Its little head twists and turns in all directions, as if the creature were searching for something.

The insect stands on its middle and back legs. It holds its front legs up, folded together in front of its "chest." The creature looks as if it were praying!

Suddenly, the insect's head stops moving. It has seen something. A grasshopper is coming toward it.

The insect darts from its hiding place. In a flash, its folded legs open up, stretch out, and snap shut on the grasshopper. The legs are like jaws with sharp teeth. They hold the startled grasshopper so that it can't move. The insect bites the back of the grasshopper's head, killing it. Then, the creature starts to eat the grasshopper. Soon, only a few scattered bits are left!

The insect is called a *mantid.* It is also known as a *praying mantis,* because it often looks as if it were praying. But when it seems to be praying, it is really hunting—and it hunts most of the time! Mantids are such fierce and greedy flesh-eaters that they are sometimes called "insect tyrannosaurs"! But they are very helpful to farmers and gardeners because they eat a great many insect pests.

A mantid will eat until it's stuffed—and then will catch another creature and start eating again! It won't hesitate to attack something bigger than it is. The largest mantids will eat birds, frogs, and small lizards. Mantids even eat other mantids. And a female mantid will usually eat the male with which she has just mated!

There are many different kinds of mantids. Most are disguised in ways that help them to hide. Many are green and blend into grass or leaves. Some look like bits of tree bark. Some are long and thin, like twigs. Some are brightly colored and hide among flowers. These mantids look so much like flowers that an insect doesn't notice them—until it is too late!

Mantids are large insects. Some kinds are as much as 5 inches (13 centimeters) long. Mantids are also one of the few kinds of insects that can be made into pets! They can be taught to take bits of raw meat or fruit from a person's fingers.

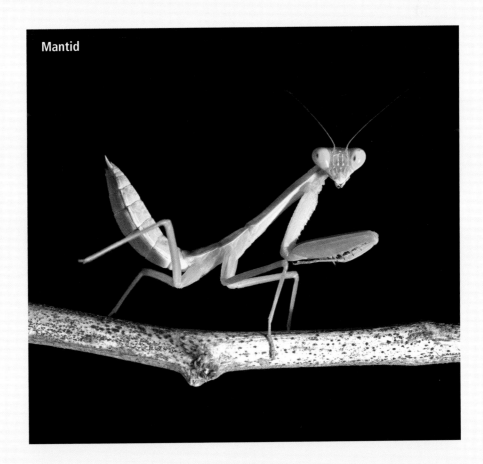

Mantid

Music makers

Crickets are the main music makers of the insect world. The steady *chirp-chirp-chirp* you often hear on a warm night is cricket music. Crickets make their music by rubbing the sharp edge on one wing against a row of bumps on the other wing.

There are many kinds of crickets. One kind, *house crickets,* likes to live in people's houses. Black, big-headed *common crickets* live in meadows and lawns, but they often come into houses. *Tree crickets* stay in trees and bushes. There are crickets that live in caves, and crickets that live in ant nests—and are fed by the ants!

Most kinds of crickets are night animals. During the day they find a place to hide. At night they come out to eat. *Field crickets* eat grass, fruits, grain, and dead insects. House crickets will eat almost any kind of food. Tree crickets eat aphids, the tiny insects that live on leaves.

Field cricket

Walkingsticks

Many people have seen what they thought was part of a bush suddenly start to walk! What they thought was a twig sticking up from a branch was really an insect that looks like a twig.

Most people call these skinny, twiglike insects *walkingsticks*. Many kinds of walkingsticks can't jump or fly, because they have no wings. They live mostly in trees or bushes.

Most kinds of walkingsticks in North America are only about 2 to 3 inches (5 to 8 centimeters) long. But in Australia there is a walkingstick about 10 inches (25 centimeters) long. And in Indonesia there is a type of walkingstick more than a foot (30 centimeters) long!

A walkingstick looks like a twig.

A "prehistoric" pest

Would you like to see a *live* "prehistoric" animal—one that lived long before the dinosaurs? Well, look at a cockroach!

There were cockroaches swarming in hot, damp forests more than 300 million years ago! And cockroaches have hardly changed a bit since. They are what scientists call a "successful living creature." This means they have not had to change their way of life for millions of years.

Many things help cockroaches survive. For one thing, a cockroach is a very fast runner. And its body is flat and slippery, so it can quickly slide into cracks that most other creatures can't get into.

Cockroaches will eat almost anything—human food, garbage, dead plants and animals, cloth, leather, even wood. This has helped them survive. An animal that eats only one thing—for example, only one certain kind of plant—doesn't have as much chance to survive as does an animal that eats many things.

Mother cockroaches don't lay "bare" eggs, as most insects do. Their eggs are protected inside a hard container that looks like a tiny purse. Some kinds of cockroaches even disguise these containers so that they look like lumps of dirt. Other types of cockroaches keep the containers with them until the eggs hatch. All this helps keep cockroach eggs from being eaten by other creatures. Some kinds of cockroaches give birth to live babies. This, too, has helped cockroaches survive.

Most kinds of cockroaches live out of doors and never come near people. During the day they hide under rocks or in the loose bark of trees. At night they come out to eat dead plants or animals.

Cockroach

But, a few kinds of cockroaches do live in houses and buildings. They, too, hide during the day. At night they come out to eat. They chew cloth, books, and other things, often ruining them. They get into people's food and spoil it. And they may spread germs.

Cockroaches are troublesome, dangerous house pests. Most people dislike them, but no one has found a good way to get rid of them. However, house cockroaches do have a few deadly enemies: one is the many-legged centipede. A centipede in the house can be a very useful friend in keeping cockroaches out.

Winged Beauties

Butterflies and moths

A fuzzy, creepy, crawly caterpillar may turn into a butterfly or it might turn into a moth. Moths and butterflies are very much alike. They both start life as caterpillars. Often, only an expert can tell if a caterpillar will turn into a butterfly or a moth.

When a caterpillar starts to change into a butterfly or moth, it becomes what is called a **pupa** *(PYOO puh)*. Sometimes, you can tell if a caterpillar will be a moth or butterfly by the way it becomes a pupa.

Most butterfly caterpillars fasten their tail to a branch or stem and hang head down. A kind of shell forms around them. This shell is called a **chrysalis** *(KRIHS uh lihs)*. Inside the chrysalis, the crawly caterpillar becomes a butterfly.

Many kinds of moth caterpillars spin a covering of silk around themselves. This covering is called a **cocoon** *(kuh KOON)*. You'll often see cocoons on tree trunks and branches, on the sides of houses, and other places. Inside each cocoon, a crawly caterpillar is becoming a moth.

When caterpillars become butterflies or moths, it's still hard to tell which is which. Butterflies and moths both have the same kind of wings and body shape. Many moths are small, brown, and not very colorful—but so are many butterflies. Many butterflies are large, brightly colored beauties—but so are many moths.

One way you can sometimes tell a butterfly from a moth is by the **antennae.** A butterfly's antennae always have a *knob,* or swelling, on the end. Most moths have antennae that either come to a point or that look like tiny feathers. No butterfly has such feathery feelers.

So, the next time you see a pair of colorful wings fluttering over a flower, don't be too sure it's a butterfly. It may be a moth. Look at its antennae and see if you can tell if it's a butterfly or a moth.

The antennae of a butterfly (above) usually have little knobs on the ends. The antennae of a moth (right) often look like feathers.

The life of a monarch caterpillar

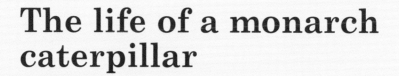

There is a flutter of color in the warm spring air. An orange and black monarch butterfly is flying northward. Below her, a young milkweed plant grows by the side of the road. Its broad leaves shiver slightly in the breeze.

The butterfly flutters down and lands on one of the milkweed leaves. She crawls around to the underside of the leaf. There she lays several eggs and coats them with something sticky so they can hold fast to the leaf.

The eggs are so tiny you would never notice them. They look like little Christmas tree ornaments. They are a gleaming yellowish-white and are covered with long rows of little bumps, like the kernels on an ear of corn.

The butterfly soars on her way. She has done her job. The eggs are in a safe place. On the underside of the leaf they are protected and hidden from creatures that might eat them. And when the babies hatch, they will have plenty of food. Milkweed leaves are what they eat.

A few days later, the first egg hatches. A pale yellowish-white caterpillar with a black head comes out of it. The caterpillar is about as thick as a bit

of thread and as long as a pinhead is wide. It has 12
eyes—6 on each side of its head. But even with
all these eyes, it can't do much more than tell light
from darkness.

The first thing the caterpillar does is eat the shell of
the egg it has come out of. Now that the shell is empty,
it looks like clear glass. The caterpillar munches on the
shell with its short, strong jaws.

Next, the caterpillar begins to eat the leaf. For the
caterpillar, the leaf is like a broad, rough meadow!
The caterpillar crawls along, munching as it goes.
As it grows, it
develops 16 stubby
legs. It crawls with
its 10 soft, lumpy
back legs. It does
not use its 6 front
legs, which are
stiff and pointed.

When a monarch caterpillar is ready to become a butterfly, it hangs head down from a twig. After a day, the caterpillar's skin begins to split. It peels away, shriveling up toward the caterpillar's tail.

As the caterpillar crawls, liquid from its mouth oozes onto the leaf. As this liquid hits the air, it becomes a thread of silk. The silk thread sticks to the leaf. As the caterpillar moves along, it leaves a trail of silk. This silken trail is important to the caterpillar. The claws on the caterpillar's feet hold on to the thread as the caterpillar crawls. It can't slip and fall as long as it has this rough, sticky path on which to walk.

The caterpillar eats and eats and grows and grows. Two days later, it has grown so much that its skin splits. The caterpillar crawls out of the skin. It waits for a while, then crawls off to start eating again.

The caterpillar keeps eating and growing and leaving its skin about every two days. Before long, it has colorful yellow, black, and white stripes. It is now big

A blue-green shell, called a chrysalis, forms around the caterpillar. It is flecked with patches of gold. For about two weeks, the chrysalis hangs from the twig. Inside the chrysalis, the caterpillar changes into a butterfly.

enough and bright enough so that it is easily seen. But, strangely, its bright colors protect it from some creatures. Most birds quickly learn that bright colors on an insect mean a bad taste. So they leave brightly colored crawlers, such as the caterpillar, alone.

But the caterpillar has one bad scare! A beetle crawls onto the leaf where the caterpillar is eating. For some beetles, a caterpillar is food! The caterpillar senses danger. At once, it lets itself fall off the leaf!

But as it falls, the liquid oozing from its mouth keeps forming silk thread. And this thread is still connected to the trail of thread on the leaf. So the caterpillar doesn't fall to the ground. It hangs by a length of thread, a short distance below the leaf. But to the beetle, the caterpillar has vanished. The beetle takes wing and flies away.

A monarch butterfly breaks out of its chrysalis after about two weeks. It clings to the chrysalis while its wings swell up and dry off. Then, it flies away.

After a time, the caterpillar climbs back up the thread. To get rid of the long piece of thread, which it no longer needs, the caterpillar eats it as it climbs! When the caterpillar reaches the leaf, it crawls on its way.

The caterpillar also has another way of protecting itself if it must. Behind its head and above its back pair of legs are two long, pointed "whips." If something touches the caterpillar, it lashes these "whips" furiously. They can't do any real damage, but they will frighten some creatures away.

After about two weeks, the caterpillar is 2 inches (5 centimeters) long. It has grown as much as it is going to.

Now it stops eating. It crawls from the leaf of the milkweed plant, where it has been living, and onto a nearby twig. It puts a little knob of sticky silk on the twig. The caterpillar attaches its tail to this knob. Then it lets itself swing out until it hangs head down from the twig.

A day goes by. The caterpillar's skin begins to split. It peels away, shriveling up toward the caterpillar's tail. But what was under the skin no longer looks like a caterpillar. It is a shapeless lump that hardens into a blue-green shell, called a *chrysalis,* that is flecked with patches of gold.

For about two weeks, the chrysalis hangs from the twig. It does not change. But inside it, tremendous changes are taking place! The caterpillar's whole body is changing into something very different!

On the 15th day, a crack appears in the chrysalis. The crack widens. Something pushes out through the crack. A struggling shape crawls out onto the chrysalis, which now looks like a piece of clear plastic.

The creature clinging to the empty chrysalis has six long legs. It also has long feelers. Its body is black, but there are orange objects on its back, like small, twisted rags.

Slowly, the "rags" swell out. They become a pair of beautiful orange and black wings, with a border of white dots. The crawling caterpillar has become a winged creature of the air—a monarch butterfly.

After a few hours, the new butterfly soars into the air. Now it begins a new kind of life.

The life of a monarch butterfly

As the new monarch butterfly wings on its way, a sweet odor attracts its attention. Following the odor, it lands on a milkweed. The plant's pinkish flowers are in bloom. Their sweet smell invites the butterfly to come and eat.

The butterfly does not eat the way it did when it was a caterpillar. The caterpillar munched bits of milkweed leaf with its powerful jaws. But the butterfly sips sweet syrup from the milkweed flowers.

These migrating monarchs, resting on a tree, will fly until they reach California, Texas, Florida, or Mexico.

The butterfly has a tongue like a long tube. This tongue is coiled up under its mouth. When the butterfly pokes its head into a flower, the tube uncoils. It becomes a long sipper that reaches down to the tiny pool of syrup at the bottom of the flower.

The butterfly spends its days flying and eating. It never walks on the ground. Its long, thin legs are too weak for walking.

Monarch butterflies live in North and South America, Australia, and a few other places. Their way of life is the same everywhere. But the North American monarchs do one thing differently. When autumn comes, all the monarchs either fly south to

Bug Bytes

Where did the monarch butterfly get its name?

Early Dutch and English settlers who came to North America were impressed by the butterfly's beautiful bright orange wings. So they named the butterfly "monarch," after William III, Prince of Orange, governor of what is now the Netherlands. William later became King of England, Scotland, and Ireland in 1689. Monarch means a king, queen, or other royal ruler. The monarch is also called "King Billy" as a nickname for King William.

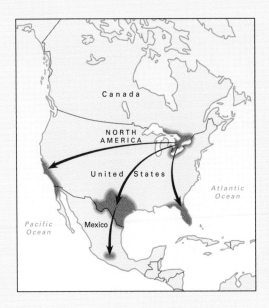

North American monarch butterflies migrate south or southwest from the northern United States and southern Canada to either California, Texas, Florida, or Mexico.

Florida or Mexico, or southwest to California or Texas. They **migrate,** just as many birds do.

So, when the sunny days grow shorter and the leaves start to change color, the butterfly heads toward warmer climates. It is joined by many others of its kind. All across the land, large flocks of monarch butterflies fly south or southwest.

At times, the butterflies stop to rest. Many thousands gather together in the same tree to spend the night. The tree looks as if it is growing butterflies from its branches, rather than leaves!

Finally, the butterfly reaches either California, Texas, Florida, or Mexico. There, too, it spends its days flying and eating. But it also mates.

After several months, the butterfly begins to move north. It does not travel in a flock, now. It flies alone.

By spring, the butterfly looks different. Its bright orange wings have become a pale tan. The butterfly does not get back to the place where it spent the last summer. On the way, it dies.

But, on their way north, many female butterflies have laid eggs. The eggs hatch into caterpillars, and the caterpillars become butterflies. These butterflies continue the journey north. And it is these butterflies that will fly south or southwest in autumn.

Caterpillars with mobile homes

Some kinds of moth caterpillars build portable homes for themselves that they carry around like a trailer! These caterpillars are known as *bagworms*. As soon as a bagworm hatches, it begins to spin a tube of silk around itself. Mixed in with the silk are bits of leaves, twigs, and dirt. Then, with only its head and first six legs sticking out of the tube, the caterpillar crawls on its way.

The tube, or bag, is quite strong and tough. It protects the caterpillar. It looks just like a bit of dirt. Hungry birds pay no attention to it. When the caterpillar has to rest, or shed its skin, it uses sticky silk to fasten the tube to something. Then it pulls its whole body inside.

A bagworm never leaves its home until it becomes a moth. As the caterpillar grows, it simply makes the tube bigger. It changes from a caterpillar to a moth inside the tube.

Bagworms are tiny. But they are big eaters and they often do a lot of damage to trees. Bagworm moths are also quite tiny. Their wingspread is only about half an inch (13 millimeters).

A bagworm inside its tube

Disguises

A caterpillar climbs slowly up a branch. The caterpillar is long and slim. Its head is reddish and its body is pale green.

The caterpillar stops crawling. It has decided to rest. It grips the branch tightly with its back pair of legs. Then it swings its body away from the branch and holds itself stiff. Suddenly, it doesn't look like a caterpillar. Its body looks like a twig on the branch. And its reddish head looks like a leaf bud.

A moth has been flying all night. Now, the sun is coming up. The moth will rest during the day.

The moth flies to a tree. It lays itself flat against the trunk, gripping the bark with the claws on its feet. The moth seems to vanish. Its speckled, brownish wings blend in perfectly with the bark on the tree.

Many kinds of caterpillars and moths can disguise themselves this way. Their bodies or wings are colored so that they blend in with leaves or bark, or look like a leaf or twig. Birds and other creatures that might eat the caterpillars and moths can't see them.

Some kinds of caterpillars have a different disguise. They are disguised to look like fierce hunting creatures. For example, the spicebush swallowtail

The spicebush swallowtail caterpillar has big eyespots that help scare away predators.

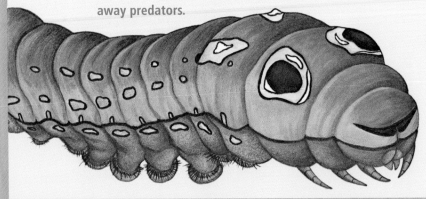

The colors on a hawk moth's wings make it blend into the bark of a tree (above). The clearwing butterfly (right) has transparent wings that make it hard to see.

caterpillar has two big spots of color high up on its back. The spots look like huge staring eyes. Many kinds of hunting creatures have large, bright eyes like this. So, it's likely that birds are frightened off by the sight of the caterpillar's "eyes" looking at them.

Some kinds of moths and butterflies also have these eye-spots on their wings. When they open their wings, the "eyes" suddenly appear. This can so startle a bird, it leaves the moth or butterfly alone.

Moth and butterfly beauties

The peacock butterfly (above) lives in temperate zones of Europe and Asia.

When the Indian leaf butterfly from Asia sits on a twig and folds its wings to show the undersides, it looks like a dead leaf (above, on the left). But the tops of its wings are colorful (right).

Luna moth

The colorful sunset moth lives on the island of Madagascar, near the east coast of Africa.

The Busy Workers

Ant babies

Sometime you may move a rock and find an ant
nest. If you kneel down and watch for a while,
you'll see an amazing sight. The ants rush about
so fast their legs seem to twinkle. Each ant picks
up what looks like a white egg and carries it out
of sight. In a short time, there isn't an ant or a
white object in sight!

Actually, the white or yellowish objects aren't
eggs. Ant eggs are tiny specks. These objects are
really baby ants. They are either ant **larvae**—
wormlike babies—or **pupae**—baby ants in
cocoons.

Ant larvae have no eyes or legs. They are fed,
cared for, and moved about by grown-up ants.
These ant "nurses" spend a lot of time licking
the babies. This feeds the babies. They also lick

Three meadow ants carry a larva.

the babies because the babies taste good. They taste good because little drops of sweet liquid ooze out of an ant larva's body.

When most kinds of ant larvae are ready to become adults, they spin a silk cocoon around themselves, just as many kinds of caterpillars do. The cocoon is oblong and cream-colored. When the new adult is ready to come out of its cocoon, an ant "nurse" often helps it.

Life in an ant nest

A female ant comes skimming out of the sky on long, rounded wings. Her black body shines in the warm summer sunlight. She lands gently in a broad meadow.

She started out in the morning, from a nest several miles or kilometers away—the nest where she was born. She will never see it again. Now she is going to start her own nest. She will be the **queen** and the mother. All the ants in the nest will be her children. While she was flying, she mated with several winged male ants from the old nest. Eggs are now growing in her body.

She begins to wiggle and rub herself against the ground. After a time, one of her wings comes off. She wiggles and rubs until the other wing breaks loose. She will never need wings again.

She begins to explore, trotting between the grass stems that rise like tall trees around her. Coming to a small, bare patch of sandy earth, she stops. Using her jaws and front feet, she begins to dig. Soon, she has made a hole big enough to lie in.

Now she lies in the hole and waits. Many months go by—nearly a year. In all that time, the young queen never eats. She gets her food from her body fat and the two big muscles on her back, where her wings were attached. These muscles slowly shrink as her body turns them into food to keep her alive.

At last, the queen begins to lay some eggs. She now needs food badly—so she eats some of the eggs. Baby ants hatch from the others. The queen feeds them with a liquid that comes from inside her body.

After a time, the babies spin cocoons around themselves and change into adults. They are all females. But they have no wings, and they will never be able to lay eggs. They are not queens like their mother.

They are workers—the first workers in the new nest.

The queen soon lays more eggs. Babies hatch out. These babies are fed by the first workers. In time, the babies become adult workers, too. They are bigger and stronger than the first workers.

The tiny nest begins to grow. The workers dig tunnels and passageways in several directions. They make special rooms to keep the larvae in. The ants dig by grabbing bits of earth with their jaws and carrying the dirt up out of the nest. Then they go back for another bit. Back and forth, and in and out, they go. They do this again and again, until the tunnel or room is finished.

While some workers dig, others care for the larvae. They feed them with their saliva and move them about to keep them cool. Still other workers scurry out of the nest in search of food, or scurry into the nest bringing in food. An ant worker is always doing some job!

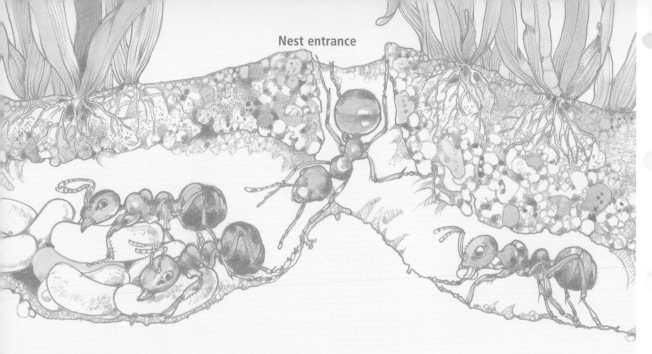

Workers caring for young

No one "tells" the workers what to do. But there are always a few workers that start doing things, and this causes other workers to join in. One or two workers may begin digging and others will quickly come to help. Or, a worker may start to move larvae to a cooler place. Then others will rush to take up the task, too.

When an ant that is exploring outside the nest finds food, she hurries back to the nest. Soon, many ants stream out of the nest, straight for the food. The worker that found the food hasn't actually "told" the others where to find it. As she returns to the nest with a bit of food, she leaves a trail of scent. The smell causes other workers to want to find food, too. All they have to do is follow the scent trail made by the first ant.

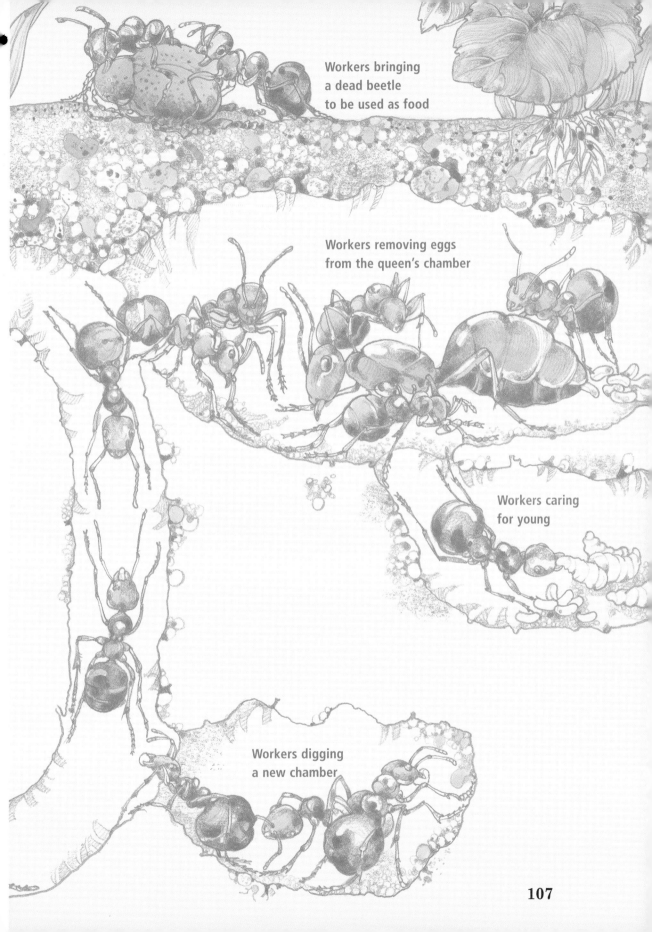

Workers bringing
a dead beetle
to be used as food

Workers removing eggs
from the queen's chamber

Workers caring
for young

Workers digging
a new chamber

107

Smell is tremendously important to the ants. Every ant in the nest has the same smell, so every ant with that smell is a "friend." When a worker enters the nest with food, all the others know she belongs there. If another worker "asks" her for some food, she can tell by smell that the other is a friend. Then she'll put some of the food she carries in her mouth into the other's mouth. But any ant or other insect with a different smell is an enemy. It will be driven away if it tries to enter the nest.

All summer long the nest is a busy, active place. But in the wintertime it is still and silent. The ants lie motionless in the cold darkness. They are alive, but their bodies are too stiff to move. They are in a kind of "frozen" sleep. In the spring, the sun warms them and they are able to move again. Once more, the ant colony bustles with activity.

Several years pass. Then, a very special day comes. Some of the queen's young have become winged females, as she once was. Others have become winged males. The time has come for these ants to leave the nest. It is like an ant holiday! As the males and females walk out of the nest, the excited workers swarm around them. One by one, the females and males soar into the air. There, they will mate. Then the females will land far away and start new nests. Thus, every ant nest is begun by an ant that has come from somewhere else.

Life in the old nest goes on for many more years. But one day the queen dies. The ant colony is doomed. No more eggs are laid. The workers die. The once bustling colony is empty and lifeless—like the ruin of an ancient city.

There are many different kinds of ants. They don't all live in the same way. Some ants make their nests in plants or out of leaves. Some do not have any nest. They simply move about from place to place. Some queens don't start their own nest—they move into an old nest, murder its queen, and take over. And some nests have more than one queen.

But all ants live in communities. There are no "hermits" in the ant world.

Farmer ants

Scurrying through the grass is what looks like a parade of ants. They trot one after the other, in a long line. Each ant carries a large piece of leaf above its head, like a green umbrella!

The ant parade goes into an underground nest. The nest is wide and deep, for it is the home of almost a million ants. There are many tunnels and rooms. Some go down as much as 20 feet (6 meters) into the ground. The nest has a thousand entrances.

The ants hurry down long, winding tunnels until they come to a large room. This room holds a number of whitish, furry-looking patches. These are about as big as the palm of your hand. The patches are the ants' farms. For these ants are farmers—*true* farmers. They grow their own food in "fields" that they water, fertilize, and weed!

These farmer ants are known as *leaf-cutter ants*. That's because they use their sharp jaws to cut bits of leaves or flowers. They carry these pieces into their nest to use as fertilizer for their fields.

The ants' crop is a **fungus**—a kind of plant that is like a mushroom or like the mold that grows on bread. The fungus grows on a stalk with a knob on the end. These knobs are the ants' food.

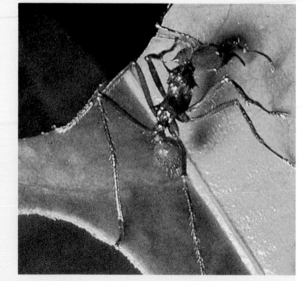

A fungus can grow in the underground darkness as long as it has water and food—which the ants give it.

The ants chew the bits of leaves and flowers into a soft, wet pulp. They put this pulp on the fields of fungus. In this way, they keep the fungus watered and fertilized.

This one kind of fungus is the leaf-cutter ants' only food. They could not live without it. And it could not grow without the care and help the ants give it.

When a young leaf-cutter queen flies off to start a new nest, she carries with her a tiny bit of fungus from the old nest. When she digs the first part of the new nest, she starts a new farm with the fungus. She takes care of it herself, until the first of her children are able to do this. Without a healthy, growing fungus farm, the new nest would be doomed.

Leaf-cutter ants use their jaws to cut curved pieces out of leaves. They use the bits of leaf as fertilizer for their underground "farms."

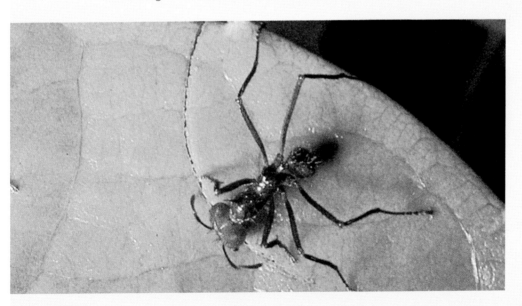

Ants that keep "cows"

In many parts of the world, people keep herds of cows, goats, or sheep for the milk they give. And there are some kinds of ants that keep herds of little insects called *aphids,* for a sweet drink the aphids give!

Aphids live on plants and are often called "plant lice." They suck the sugary juice that's in the leaves, stems, and roots of plants. A lot of the juice they eat simply goes right through them and drips out of their bodies.

Many kinds of ants love this sweet juice. They run about on leaves, licking up drops of the juice that aphids leave behind. Often, an ant will "milk" an aphid, much as a person milks a cow. The ant does this by rubbing its feelers against the aphid's body. Then the aphid lets a drop of the sweet juice, called **honeydew,** ooze out of its body for the ant to lick up.

For some kinds of ants, aphid honeydew is the main food. These ants really do protect and take care of aphids, much as people look after herds of cows! This is why they are called *dairying ants.*

One kind of dairying ant lives in cornfields in parts of the United States and Canada. Their aphids feed on the roots of corn plants. In the fall, when the aphids lay eggs, the ants gather up the eggs. They carry the eggs into their underground nest to protect them during winter.

In the spring, the ants bring out the eggs to hatch. When the eggs hatch, the ants carry the young aphids to the roots of young corn plants. The aphids feed on the roots and make honeydew. This is fine for the ants, but it kills the corn.

When a young queen ant flies off to begin a new colony, she carries with her a mother aphid that's ready to lay eggs.

When the queen starts her colony, her ants will have their own herd of aphids!

Masters and slaves

It is an ordinary day at a nest of silky ants. Some workers trot out to look for food. Others come in with bits of food they've found. Inside the nest, certain workers, the "nurses," care for the babies. Other workers fuss around the queen.

Suddenly, outside the nest, a large group of different ants appears. These ants have bright, shiny red bodies. The red ants move boldly toward the silky ant nest.

It is an attacking army! The attackers swarm into the nest. The silky ants fight to defend their home. But they cannot beat the red ants. The long, curved jaws of the red ants are terrible weapons.

The red ants charge through the tunnels. Killing any "nurse" that tries to stop them, they seize the baby silky ants. Then they rush back through the

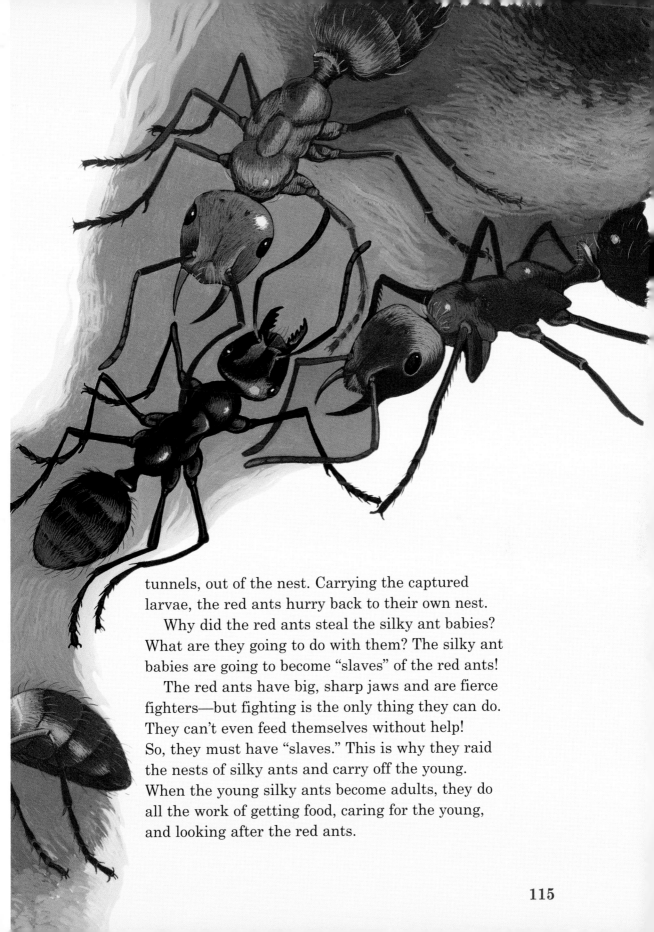

tunnels, out of the nest. Carrying the captured larvae, the red ants hurry back to their own nest.

Why did the red ants steal the silky ant babies? What are they going to do with them? The silky ant babies are going to become "slaves" of the red ants!

The red ants have big, sharp jaws and are fierce fighters—but fighting is the only thing they can do. They can't even feed themselves without help! So, they must have "slaves." This is why they raid the nests of silky ants and carry off the young. When the young silky ants become adults, they do all the work of getting food, caring for the young, and looking after the red ants.

A red queen doesn't dig a nest, as most young ant queens do. She simply looks for a nest of silky ants and marches into it. When she finds the queen, she kills her and becomes the new queen of the nest!

The silky ants treat the red queen just as they treat their own queen. When she starts laying eggs, they care for the eggs just as they would their own. They treat the red ants that hatch just as they treat each other.

In time, there are fewer silky ants, because none of their kind of eggs are being laid. That's when the red ants begin to raid other silky ant nests, to capture more "slaves." So, a red ant nest is home to two different kinds of ants—red ants who can't do anything but fight, and silky ants who do all the work.

Bug Bytes

A jaw-dropping, acrobatic ant

The great white shark has nothing on the tiny trap-jaw ant. This insect has the mightiest mandibles of any animal on Earth!

The half-inch (1.25-centimeter) ant, found in Central and South America, uses its strong, lightning-fast jaws to clamp shut on prey, such as other ants or termites, in less than a millisecond—that's faster than anything else found in nature!

But it can also use its jaws to escape predators! When frightened, the ant snaps its jaws shut to flip itself backwards into the air, somersaulting end-over-end like a gymnast to land 15 inches (38 centimeters) away! That's the equivalent of a 5-foot-6-inch (168-centimeter) person jumping 132 feet (40 meters)!

Harvester ants

Harvesters are people who gather up the ripe crops in late summer and fall. Some kinds of ants are known as *harvesters*. When the seeds of many plants grow ripe and plump, the ants gather them up and bring them into the nest. The ants eat some of the seeds right away. But they also store seeds in the nest. This way they always have food when they can't find fresh seeds.

Most seeds the ants bring into the nest are still in their husks, or shells. The ants take the seeds out of the husks and store them. Then they carry the husks up out of the nest and throw them away. You can often tell where a harvester ant nest is by the wide ring of seed husks lying all around it.

Sometimes the stored seeds get damp. Then workers will carry them all outside and put them in the sunshine to dry.

A conquering army

A raiding army is moving through a forest. Every living creature in its path is in deadly danger. The soldiers of this army will kill any creature that can't get away!

By the tens of thousands, the soldiers swarm among the trees. There are so many of them they completely blanket the ground. Their weapons are their jaws, which are like curved, sharp swords. These soldiers are ants, and they are seeking food.

A dozen of the soldiers come upon a beetle larva. In an instant, it is torn to bits. Other soldiers find a sick lizard that can't move.

It is hundreds of times bigger than an ant, but the ants swarm over it by the thousands. It, too, is cut to pieces. Any animal that can't get out of the path of the raiders is doomed. Even a large animal, such as a cow, can be chewed to bits until only the bones are left!

Army ants, as this kind of ant is called, do not have a regular nest. Every 2 to 3 weeks, army ants "make camp," perhaps beneath the roots of a tree. There, they huddle in a huge, glistening cluster. For about nine days, the queen lays eggs—thousands of them. Meanwhile, thousands of baby ants lie wrapped in cocoons, changing into adults.

After another 10 days or so, the eggs have hatched. At the same time, the babies that have now become adults begin to break out of their cocoons. Both the babies and the new adults are fiercely hungry—and they must have meat! So, the army moves off in search of food.

The horde of ants moves mostly by night. The babies are carried by workers. The big-headed, sharp-jawed soldiers move at the front and sides of the army. The queen marches along near the rear. She is bigger than all the other ants and is always surrounded by a crowd of workers.

This army of ants cannot see where it is going. Most kinds of army ants are blind. However, as each ant moves, it leaves a scent trail behind it. So, each ant simply follows the trail of the ants ahead. The ants at the front have no trail to follow, of course. They just move forward blindly, pushed along by those behind them.

The army halts by day. This is when the swarms or columns of raiders move out in search of food. Every insect, spider, worm, animal, or bird the soldiers run into is attacked at once. Many creatures are eaten on the spot. Others are torn to bits and the pieces carried back to the rest of the army.

After about three weeks, most of the army is well fed. The babies are beginning to spin cocoons around themselves. So, once again, the army halts and "makes camp." Once again, the queen begins to lay eggs.

Guests and pests

You'd be horrified if your family invited guests into your home—and let the guests eat you! But that's what some ants do!

In many ant nests there are often a number of *claviger* beetles. These beetles can make a liquid ooze out of a place on their back. The ants love this liquid. An ant will often stroke the beetle, which then makes a drop of the liquid for the ant to lick up. Then the ant feeds the beetle by spitting up some of its digested food. So the ants and the beetles are happy dining together!

However, some of the beetles aren't always satisfied with plain ant food. Sometimes they eat ant eggs and ant babies. And the ants let them do it! It seems that as long as the beetles supply their sweet liquid, the ants let them do what they please.

There are often many different creatures in an ant nest. But they're not all welcome guests like the beetles. Many of them are pests and thieves.

Some of these pests are *mites*. Mites are tiny, eight-legged creatures related to spiders. A mite will fasten itself onto an ant, usually close to the ant's head. The ant can't get the mite off, so it has to carry the mite everywhere. Whenever the ant gives food to or gets food from another ant—the mite reaches out and steals some!

An ant (top) feeds a beetle.

The wood eaters

In an old house, some of the wooden boards begin to crumble away. An old, dead tree suddenly splits and crashes to the ground. A thick piece of timber supporting a bridge suddenly gives way and the bridge collapses. When such things happen, chances are that termites have been at work!

Termites are insects that eat wood. In North America, communities of termites live in dead trees and in the wooden parts of houses. The termites eat many long, branching tunnels in the wood around their nest. In time, the wood becomes almost hollow. What looks like a solid tree or board may be as thin as paper!

Although termites eat wood, they can't digest it as we digest our food. Tiny, one-celled creatures that live in the termites' stomachs do this for them.

Termites are often called "white ants," but they aren't even closely related to ants. They're more like cockroaches. However, like ants, they live in communities.

At certain times, swarms of winged male and female termites fly from an old nest. When a male and female find one another, they dig a small, hidden nest.

After a time, the female lays her first eggs. The babies that hatch have six legs and can run about. These baby termites don't spin cocoons to become adults. They simply keep growing and shedding their skins. In time, most become adult workers or soldiers. Some become winged adults.

The termite workers are small and have soft, pale bodies. Their small jaws are good only for digging or carrying things. But the soldiers are big, with large, hard heads and long, sharp jaws that are deadly weapons. Some kinds of termites have both workers and soldiers in the nest, but some kinds have only soldiers.

Most kinds of termite workers and soldiers are blind. But they don't really need eyes. Most of them never leave the nest, which is completely dark.

Termites eat tunnels in the wood around their nest.

A termite city

On the plains of East Africa there are many strange reddish towers. These towers rise as high as 20 feet (6 meters). They look a bit like lumpy pyramids. If you were to touch one, you would find it is as hard as rock. These strange towers are termite nests.

An African termite tower is an amazing place. It is home for nearly a million termites! Each tower is a sealed-up "city" of many tunnels and rooms. There is even a great "garden," for these termites are "farmers" and raise most of their own food. This food is a simple plant, called *fungus,* that can grow in the dark.

The termite city is ruled by a queen and a king. It is guarded by an army of fierce soldiers. And it is kept running by a host of busy, active workers.

The workers do all kinds of tasks. They dig new tunnels. They build new walls with sand and clay brought up from below the ground. They tend the gardens, where the city's food is grown. They feed the queen, king, babies, and soldiers. They take care of the queen's eggs.

The soldiers don't do anything but fight. So, most of the time they have nothing to do. They usually just wander around the nest, begging for food. Because the soldiers aren't able to feed themselves, the workers have to feed them. Sometimes, if a nest has too many soldiers and not enough food, some of the soldiers are put to death! They are simply starved to death—no worker will give them any food.

But there are times when the soldiers are needed. The termites have a bitter enemy—ants! At times, ants from a nearby nest, or perhaps a horde of army ants, will break into the tower. Then the termite soldiers rush into battle. They will fight to the death to drive off the invaders.

Tiny African termites nest inside
huge mounds that they build.

Termites and ants are enemies.
This ant attacks a termite soldier.

The termite queen does nothing but lay eggs. She lays thousands of eggs a day! In order to produce so many eggs, she has to eat almost all the time. As the eggs multiply inside her, she swells up. Some kinds of termite queens swell up so much they look like a small sausage, as much as 4 inches (10 centimeters) long and an inch (2.5 centimeters) wide! Such a queen is nearly 2,000 times bigger than a tiny worker. She is so heavy she can't move.

A swarm of workers always surrounds the queen. They bring her food and lick her body. And there is always a crowd of other termites moving in and out of her chamber.

There are even "police" termites on hand, to keep the crowd from getting too close to the queen. It is almost as if the queen's subjects want to be near her, just as people often want to be near some famous or important person.

As long as the queen can lay eggs, she is the most important termite in the nest. But when she gets too old, she is doomed. The workers stop giving her food and lick her to death! A young female termite is then chosen as the new queen. She mates with the old king and starts laying eggs.

All this happens in complete darkness. Termites dislike light, and most of them never leave the nest. Sometimes, workers must go outside to find new soil for the fungus garden. Then, they build long tunnels of mud to protect themselves from sunlight.

A termite queen does nothing but lay eggs. Workers feed her. She becomes as large and fat as a small sausage.

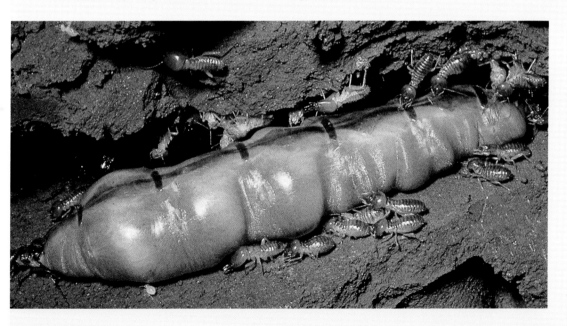

Honey Makers

The way of the honey bee

It is springtime, and an apple tree has burst into bloom. Its blossoms are puffs of white against bright green leaves. But a honey bee buzzing about nearby sees the blossoms as bright blue-green spots against a background of yellow leaves! The color and smell of the blossoms are a signal to the bee. This is how she knows the tree has something for her.

She alights on one of the blossoms and pushes down into it. Stretching out her tongue, which is like a long tube, she sucks up the bit of sweet **nectar** inside the flower. She flits from one blossom to another, sucking up more nectar. Soon, the little sack, or *honey stomach,* inside her body is full.

All the time the bee is getting the nectar, she is also doing something important for the tree. As she pushes into each flower, she gets a yellowish powder, called **pollen,** all over her hairy body. Some of this pollen rubs off in each flower she visits. Pollen from one flower makes seeds start to grow in another flower. In this way, the bee helps the flowers make seeds from which new apple trees will grow.

The bee also collects some of the pollen for food. She scrapes some of it off herself and mixes it with a tiny bit of nectar, to make sticky lumps. She pushes these golden lumps into "baskets" of stiff hairs on her back legs.

When her "baskets" and honey stomach are full, the bee no longer flies here and there in search of flowers. Now, she heads straight home, making a beeline for her **hive.** The hive, which is in a hollow tree, is home for some 50,000 bees. Most of them are workers. But there is one **queen** bee. She does nothing but lay eggs.

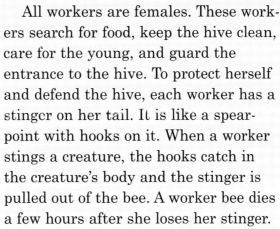

All workers are females. These workers search for food, keep the hive clean, care for the young, and guard the entrance to the hive. To protect herself and defend the hive, each worker has a stinger on her tail. It is like a spearpoint with hooks on it. When a worker stings a creature, the hooks catch in the creature's body and the stinger is pulled out of the bee. A worker bee dies a few hours after she loses her stinger.

Reaching the hollow tree, the bee goes past some guard bees and through a large crack in the trunk. Hanging down inside the tree are a number of long, thick strips of wax. These are the **honeycombs.** Each comb is made up of thousands of tiny "rooms," or cells, all joined together. Thousands of workers built these combs out of bits of wax that came from their bodies.

Honey in cells

Workers sharing nectar

Larvae

Queen surrounded by workers

Wax-covered cells

Young queen's cells

When a bee finds a place to get nectar, she flies straight home. In the nest, she does a "dance" that shows other bees how to find the nectar. She trots in straight lines and scurries in circles. The straight lines show the direction to take. The circles show the distance to the nectar.

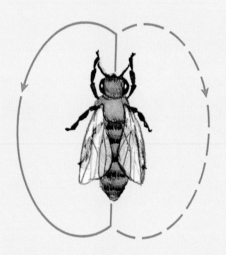

The six-sided cells are store-rooms. Many are filled with honey or with pollen—food for the bees. In some cells there are long, slim eggs. In others, there are little, wormlike baby bees. Still other cells are covered with wax lids. In these cells lie baby bees wrapped in silk **cocoons.** These babies are changing into adults.

The bee that found the apple tree alights on part of a comb that has many empty cells. At once, she is surrounded by other workers. Several stretch out their tongues to her. She brings up nectar from her honey stomach. Each one sucks up some of it. But they don't eat it. One worker scurries off to feed the nectar to a baby bee. Others put their nectar into empty cells. In a few days, it will thicken into honey.

Meanwhile, the bee that brought the nectar begins an odd sort of "dance." She does her "dance" over and over again, while the other workers swarm excitedly around her. She is showing them where the apple tree is. Each time she makes a straight line, she is pointing the direction to the tree. And the speed at which she makes circles shows the distance to the tree.

Soon, many workers are winging toward the apple tree. Some fill themselves with nectar. Others collect only pollen. When the "baskets" on their legs are filled, these bees fly back to the hive. There, they scrape the pollen into empty cells in the honeycombs.

When a cell is filled, other workers take over. They let wax ooze out of their bodies. They chew it until it is soft and then use it to make wax covers for all of the pollen-filled cells.

Workers hatch from most of the queen's eggs. But a few baby queens hatch. And some males hatch. Soon, these babies start to spin cocoons around themselves. This seems to be a signal. Suddenly, the queen and many of the workers rush out of the hive! They fly away in a great

A baby queen bee changes into an adult in a cell shaped a bit like a peanut. The first queen to break out of her cell becomes the hive's new queen.

swarm. They will start a new hive somewhere else. Never again will they return to the hollow tree.

About half the workers are left behind. They go about their work as usual. But now there is no queen.

After about 10 days, one of the young queens becomes an adult and breaks out of her cocoon. She searches for every cell in which there is another young queen in a cocoon. One by one, she kills all the others! She is the hollow tree's new queen, and she wants no rivals! She does her killing with her smooth, curved stinger, which is used only to kill other queens. Unlike a worker, a queen does not lose her stinger when she uses it. Nor does she die afterward.

The **drones** (males) are also adults now. They don't do any work. They have no stinger. Their only purpose in life is to mate with a young queen.

After a few days, the queen and all the drones leave the hive. As the drones follow, the queen flies higher and higher. Finally, one drone reaches her, and they mate. Then the drone dies. The queen and the other drones return to the hive. After a time, the queen begins to lay eggs.

Spring turns into summer. Each day, the busy worker bees search the land around the hollow tree for nectar and pollen. Some of this is eaten by the workers or fed to the **larvae** (young), the queen, and the drones. But a lot of the nectar is stored away as food for the winter.

Young workers do most of the work inside the hive. The youngest spend their time cleaning out pits, so that the queen can lay eggs in them. Young workers also feed the babies. As a worker grows older, she becomes a builder, making and repairing combs with the wax from her body. The oldest workers hunt for food. During the summer, a worker lives only about six weeks after becoming an adult.

In autumn, the bees begin to get ready for winter. One of the first things they do is to push all the drones out of the hive. The drones are left to starve to death because they are of no use now.

The queen lays fewer and fewer eggs. Finally, she lays no eggs at all. As the inside of the nest grows colder, the workers bunch together on both sides of a honey-filled comb. They form a big crowd, with the queen in the middle.

All winter long, the bees stay pressed together. But they keep moving and wiggling their wings. From time to time, they take sips of honey to keep up their energy. The heat of their bodies and their movements keep them fairly warm. Most of them live through the winter. And when spring comes, the life of the hive will start up again.

Fossil bee in amber

Bug Bytes

Interesting facts about bees

- A fossil bee found trapped in amber probably lived 80 million years ago.
- The largest bee is *Chalicodoma pluto,* a mason bee about 1¼ inches (3.8 centimeters) long. The largest honey bee, called the giant honey bee, or Asian rock bee, is about 1 inch (2.5 centimeters) long.
- The smallest bee is *Trigona minima,* a stingless bee only 1/12 inch (2 millimeters) long. The dwarf bee, the smallest honey bee, is under ½ inch (13 millimeters).
- A strong, healthy colony may contain between 50,000 and 60,000 bees.
- Worker bees fly about 15 miles (24 kilometers) per hour.
- Honey bees can identify a flavor as sweet, sour, salty, or bitter.
- A worker honey bee collects enough nectar in its lifetime to make about 1/10 pound (45 grams) of honey.

Bumble bees

Bumble bees are usually bigger and sturdier than honey bees. They live in an underground nest, which is often in an old mouse hole. Like honey bees, they collect nectar and make honey. But they don't store the honey in wax combs. They save their old cocoons and store their honey in them.

A bumble bee queen starts a nest by herself in the spring. She makes a tiny "pot" out of wax from her body. Into this, she puts a ball of pollen and nectar. She lays eggs in the pollen ball. When the baby bees hatch, they're lying on their food.

The queen lays eggs during the summer. Most of the babies become workers and gather food. But not much food is needed. At summer's end, all the bees die.

During late summer, young queens and males hatch from some of the eggs. They fly off and mate. In winter, young bumble bee queens hide in the ground. In the spring, they come out and life starts again.

Unlike honey bees, bumble bees do not lose their stinger or die after using it. Bumble bees can sting again and again.

The yellowish balls are cocoons in a bumble bee nest (right). After the young bees come out of them, workers use the empty cocoons for storing honey and pollen.

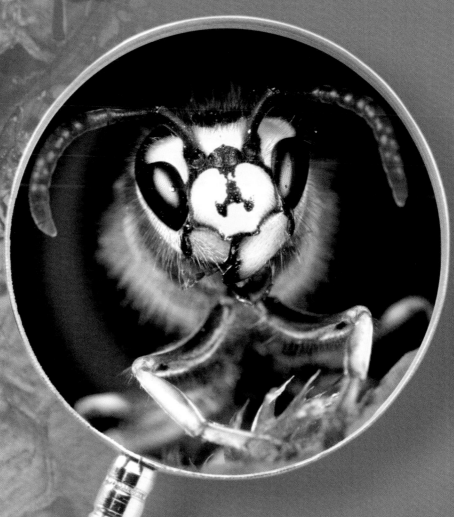

Hunters and
Builders

The hunting wasp

The female wasp buzzing among the flowers seemed quite harmless. She spent her days sipping **nectar** from flowers and basking in the sunshine. Caterpillars and other insects crawled about, but she paid no attention to them. She preferred the nectar.

One day she began to dig in the ground. She dug with her jaws, lifting up bits of dirt and putting them in a pile. She worked slowly and carefully. After several hours, her work was finished. She had made a short tunnel with a round room at the end.

Picking up a clump of dirt, she sealed off the entrance to the tunnel. Carefully, she smoothed out the dirt around the entrance. She wanted to hide all signs of her work so that no other creature could find the nest.

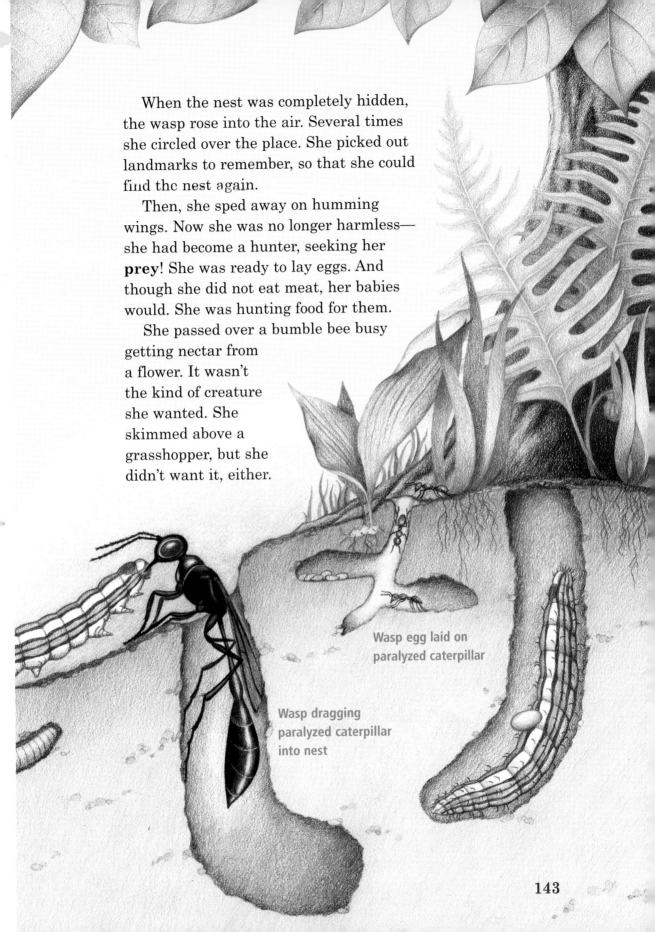

When the nest was completely hidden, the wasp rose into the air. Several times she circled over the place. She picked out landmarks to remember, so that she could find the nest again.

Then, she sped away on humming wings. Now she was no longer harmless—she had become a hunter, seeking her **prey**! She was ready to lay eggs. And though she did not eat meat, her babies would. She was hunting food for them.

She passed over a bumble bee busy getting nectar from a flower. It wasn't the kind of creature she wanted. She skimmed above a grasshopper, but she didn't want it, either.

Wasp egg laid on paralyzed caterpillar

Wasp dragging paralyzed caterpillar into nest

Then she saw a large caterpillar crawling on a leaf. This was her prey!

She swooped onto the caterpillar's back. At once, it began to jerk and hump its back, like a wild horse trying to throw off a rider. But the wasp clamped her jaws onto the caterpillar's head and hung on tightly. The long, sharp stinger in her tail stabbed down into the caterpillar's body. The caterpillar stopped moving.

The caterpillar wasn't dead. The poison from the wasp's stinger hadn't killed it. But the caterpillar was paralyzed and could not move. The wasp stung the caterpillar several more times. Now the caterpillar would not be able to move for a long time.

The wasp began to drag the caterpillar back to the nest she had dug. It was hard work. The caterpillar was bigger and heavier than she. But, finally, she reached the nest.

It took the wasp a few moments to find the hidden entrance to the nest. Quickly, she dug it open. Grabbing the caterpillar's head in her jaws, she dragged the

caterpillar into the room at the end of the tunnel.
She laid a tiny egg on the caterpillar's back. Then she
scrambled out of the nest and sealed it up again.

She then flew away. During the next few days she
would dig more nests and hunt more caterpillars to
put in them.

A few days later, a tiny, wormlike baby wasp
hatched in the dark nest. It had plenty of food—a
whole caterpillar hundreds of times bigger than it.

Day after day, the baby ate and grew. In time, it
ate the whole caterpillar. Then it spun a silk **cocoon**
around itself.

By now, fall had come. All through fall and winter,
the young wasp stayed wrapped in its cocoon. By the
time spring came, the wasp was an adult. It broke out
of the cocoon, dug its way out of the nest, and flew
off. Now it searched for nectar from flowers. And if it
was a female, it would someday hunt caterpillars for
its babies.

There are many different kinds of hunting wasps.
Each kind hunts a different kind of prey. Some hunt
beetles, some hunt flies, some hunt bees, some catch
grasshoppers, some catch different kinds of caterpillars. One kind even hunts big tarantula spiders.

A nest of paper

An old log lay among a pile of dead leaves in a woods. A small winged creature came gliding through the air toward it—a young female hornet. She hovered a moment, then alighted beside the log. She crept beneath it and settled herself among the leaves.

It was late autumn, and the weather soon turned cold. Winter arrived, with its snowstorms and freezing days. The weather was often bitterly cold. The hornet lay motionless as the winter months passed.

In time, the air grew warmer. Spring sunshine filled the woods. One day, the hornet began to move. She wiggled her **antennae.** She twitched her wings. After a while, she flew up and circled about, looking around the woods. Last autumn she had mated. Now she wanted a good place to make a nest and start laying her eggs.

Settling on a tree, she scraped off a tiny bit of bark with her jaws. She chewed it into a wet paste. Then she flew up to a branch. She stuck the bit of paste onto the underside of the branch.

Back and forth she went, from the trunk of the tree to the branch, again and again. Each time, she added a bit of wood paste. She built a little cup, hanging down from a stem fastened to the branch. The paste quickly dried into a stiff, tough, grayish paper. The hornet made several more paper cups, all joined together. Then she put a paper covering around them, with a hole in the bottom for an entrance.

In each of the cups, the hornet laid an egg. The eggs were sticky and stuck to the bottom of the cups.

A hornet's nest is opened to show the inside. The yellowish shapes are larvae. Some cells have silk covers spun by older larvae. After about 10 days, they tear off the covers and come out as adults. The queen hornet laid the tiny egg in the center cell.

Days passed, and the eggs began to hatch. Little wormlike babies came out of the eggs. Each baby hung head downward, attached to its cup by a sort of glue that oozed out of the back of its body.

The babies had to be fed, and their food was fresh meat. The mother hornet went hunting and killed a caterpillar. She chewed up bits of it and brought these to the babies. For a while, she spent most of her time bringing food to the babies.

The babies began to grow longer and fatter. Soon, they were so fat they didn't need glue to hold them in their cups—they fit so tightly that they couldn't fall out!

The mother hornet worked hard caring for her young. But after a time, some of the fat babies spun silk covers over their cups. Inside the covered cups,

A hornet worker is adding paper to the outside
of the nest. She chews wood into a ball of paste.
Then she spreads the paste on the nest.

they began to change into adults. Before long, there
were a number of grown-up daughters to begin helping
their mother.

The daughters hunted insects and nectar, fed the
babies, and worked on the nest. They added more
groups of cups, covering them with walls of paper.
The nest soon became a large oval ball.

All summer long, the nest bustled with activity.
Thousands of hornets made it their home. Most were
female workers. By the late summer, though, some
males and some "princesses," who would someday be
queens, had hatched.

By early autumn, the nest was dying. The males
and the princesses flew away to mate. They did
not come back. The old queen died. No more eggs

were laid. Then the workers, too, began to die. By late autumn, the nest was silent and empty.

The insects we call *hornets* are really a kind of wasp. Many kinds of wasps and hornets live in hanging nests made of paper. But the hornets known as *yellow jackets* usually make their nests underground.

Bug Bytes

Wasp wannabes

Wasps are known for their painful sting. So other, stingless insects have evolved to look like them!

A stingless syrphid fly (top) mimics the colors and patterns of a stinging wasp (bottom). This gives the unprotected insect a chance to outwit enemies that think it is a stinging wasp!

True Bugs, Hoppers, and Fleas

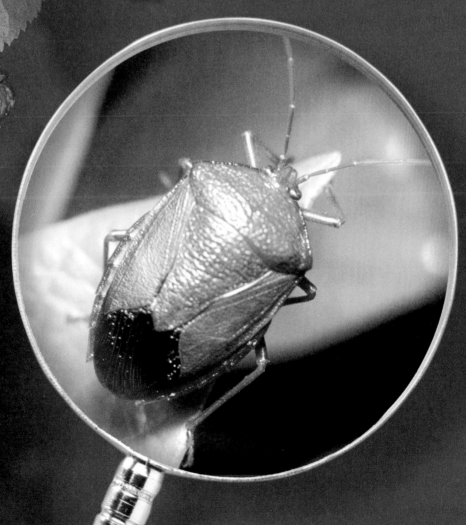

Insect skunks

Stink bugs are the skunks of the insect world. When a stink bug is in danger, it sprays a bad-smelling and bad-tasting liquid out of openings near its back legs. This keeps a bird or other animal from eating it.

There are many kinds of stink bugs. Most kinds have bodies shaped like the shields used by knights of old. In the United Kingdom, stink bugs are usually called *shieldbugs*. Many kinds of stink bugs are brightly colored, but some look like bits of bark. Some are the color of leaves.

A great many kinds of stink bugs are harmful pests that spoil vegetables and fruit. But some stink bugs are helpful. They eat harmful caterpillars and other insects.

Stink bugs are members of the group of insects scientists call **bugs.** We often call any insect or tiny creature a bug. But true bugs are a particular group of insects. All true bugs have a sharp beak for a mouth.

Some bugs are tiny, and some are large. Some have wings; some do not. Most bugs live on land, but some live in water. Some true bugs, such as stink bugs and water bugs, have "bug" as part of their name. But other "bugs," such as Junebugs and potato bugs, belong to the beetle group. They are not true bugs.

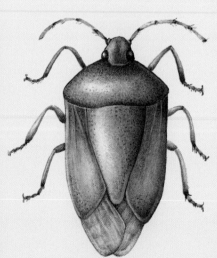

Most stink bugs have a body shaped like a shield.

Water walkers

The bug known as a *water strider, sea skater,* or *pond-skater* can stand, run, and even jump on the surface of the water in a quiet pond or pool. For the water strider, the surface is like a thin, rubbery "skin" over the rest of the water. The water strider's feet make little dents in the "skin," but they don't break through it.

When a water strider runs, it looks as if it is skating. It uses only four legs for running—the two middle ones and the two back ones. It uses its front legs like arms, to grab smaller insects. When it catches another insect, it jabs its sharp beak into the creature's body and sucks it dry.

Some kinds of water striders live on rivers. A few kinds even live on the ocean. But none of these creatures can swim. And most of them will drown if they happen to get into the water.

This water strider's feet make little dents as it walks on the surface of the water.

Hoppers

Have you ever seen a thorn on a twig suddenly come to life and hop away? If so, it was really an insect—the kind called a *hopper*. Hoppers are hard to see, even when you're looking right at one. They're small and often look like part of the plant they're sitting on.

There are many kinds of hoppers. The ones known as *treehoppers* are also called *thorn bugs*. The hard skin on a thorn bug's back forms a high, curved point that looks just like a thorn. It is usually colored green or brown. When a thorn bug squats on a twig, it looks like a thorn.

Froghoppers sometimes look like tiny, big-eyed, green or brown tree frogs. They're also called *spittle-bugs*. Mother spittlebugs lay eggs on grass stems in the fall. In the spring, the young spittlebugs hatch.

Many kinds of treehoppers look just like a thorn when they sit on a twig. Because of this, these insects are known as thorn bugs.

After it hatches, a spittlebug larva covers itself with a foamy, sticky liquid that looks like spit. This protects it from sunlight and from most enemies.

After a spittlebug hatches, the **larva** stands head downward on a blade of grass. It then squirts a mixture of air and sticky liquid out of its body. This bubbly, foamy stuff looks like spit—which is why this bug is called a spittlebug. The foamy stuff slides down over the spittlebug's body, covering it completely.

The spittlebug stays inside this foamy "tent" until it grows up. It eats by sipping juice out of the grass stem. The sticky foam protects it from most enemies and from the hot sun.

Leafhoppers usually have a green or greenish-yellow body. When they crouch on a leaf, they can hardly be noticed. But some kinds of leafhoppers are brightly colored and easy to see.

Hoppers got their name because they do a lot of hopping. They can make long, powerful leaps from one plant to another. They can also fly.

All hoppers are juice suckers that feed on many kinds of plants. They cause the plants they feed on to wilt, to stop growing, and to catch diseases that kill them. Hoppers spoil potatoes, beets, celery, grapes, and many other plants people use for food.

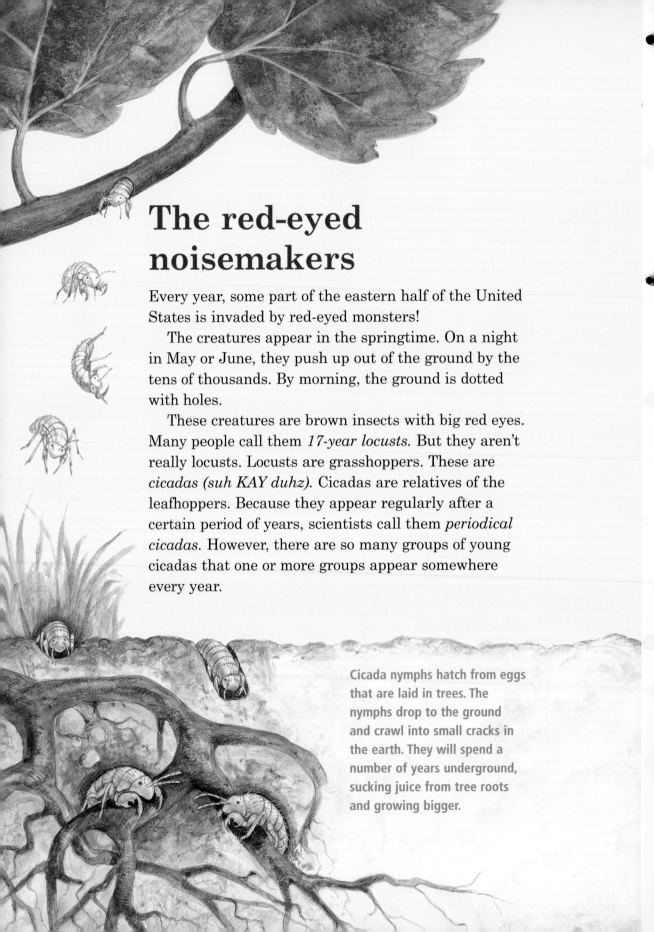

The red-eyed noisemakers

Every year, some part of the eastern half of the United States is invaded by red-eyed monsters!

The creatures appear in the springtime. On a night in May or June, they push up out of the ground by the tens of thousands. By morning, the ground is dotted with holes.

These creatures are brown insects with big red eyes. Many people call them *17-year locusts*. But they aren't really locusts. Locusts are grasshoppers. These are *cicadas (suh KAY duhz)*. Cicadas are relatives of the leafhoppers. Because they appear regularly after a certain period of years, scientists call them *periodical cicadas*. However, there are so many groups of young cicadas that one or more groups appear somewhere every year.

Cicada nymphs hatch from eggs that are laid in trees. The nymphs drop to the ground and crawl into small cracks in the earth. They will spend a number of years underground, sucking juice from tree roots and growing bigger.

The instant a cicada leaves the ground, it heads straight for the nearest tree. Soon, all the nearby trees are filled with the little creatures. If there are no trees, the cicadas will climb onto bushes, weeds, or even blades of grass. When the cicadas come out of the ground, they're not quite grown-up. They go into the trees and stay there until they are adults.

Each cicada clings to its perch and begins to hump its back. The skin splits down the back, and the young cicada struggles out. It is yellowish-white, with two black spots on its back behind its red eyes. Slowly, two ragged bumps on its back swell up and become soft, white wings.

After a time, the cicada's body turns gray, then black. The wings become clear, shiny, and yellow, with orange veins in them. The cicada is now an adult and ready for life. For a female, this means mating and laying eggs. For a male, it mostly means making noise!

The cicada nymphs tunnel up out of the ground. They head for trees or bushes. Each nymph sheds its skin and becomes a winged adult. In time, the adults mate. The females lay eggs in branches and the cycle starts again.

Soon after a cicada nymph comes out of the ground, its skin splits open. The cicada crawls out of the old skin (bottom) as a winged adult.

A few days after they become adults, the male cicadas begin to "sing" to attract females. The males sing all day long, and all together, by the thousands! The sound is a steady *bur-r-r* that some people find very annoying. Fortunately, the cicadas don't sing at night— or it might be impossible for people to sleep!

A male periodical cicada makes noise the same way a drum does. And part of the cicada's body is like a drum. At the middle of the cicada's body, on each side, is an oval patch of thin skin. The cicada's body is hollow between the patches. The patches of stretched skin and the hollow body form a drum. The cicada "beats" the drum by making the skin patches vibrate.

A few days after a female mates, she begins laying eggs. At the end of her body she has a long, sharp tube. She uses this tube to bore rows of little slits in twigs. In each slit she lays about 20 white, oblong eggs. Unfortunately, when there are a lot of female cicadas laying eggs, they often cause great damage, especially to young trees.

For several weeks, the singing, the mating, and the egg laying go on. Then, the cicadas begin to die. Soon, the ground beneath the trees is strewn with their bodies. The noise of the males' drums is heard no more.

After a few more weeks, the eggs in the twigs begin to hatch. The tiny **nymphs** have feelers and six legs. But when they hatch, they are wrapped in tight-fitting bags of skin they must first wiggle out of. Each nymph scurries along the twig, then drops off or is blown off, and drifts to the ground. Quickly, it goes underground, through the first crack in the earth it finds.

The nymph pushes down until it is 1 or 2 feet (30 to 60 centimeters) underground. It finds a tree root into which it pushes its beak. Depending upon what kind of cicada it is, it will spend from 4 to 17 years there, sucking juice from the root and growing. Then, one spring evening it will dig its way up out of the ground. And soon, there will be a brand-new horde of red-eyed noisemakers.

Bug Bytes

Fish-eating bug!

Some bugs are very large. The giant water bug grows as big as 2 ⅓ inches (6 centimeters)!

Giant water bugs are fierce hunters and will chase after fish, frogs, salamanders, and other creatures bigger than themselves. Some are known as *toe biters,* because they nip at the toes of people who swim in their pond!

Insect vampires

Fleas are insect vampires. They live on dogs, cats, birds, and other animals—and sometimes on people—and suck their blood!

A flea is a strange-looking creature. It has a very small head and no wings. Its sides are flat, so that it is like a coin standing on edge. This enables the flea to move easily between the hair or feathers on an animal's body. For the flea, this must be like walking through a forest of small trees that are growing close together.

You might think that when a dog or cat scratches itself, its claw would easily push the fleas out of its fur. But all over a flea's back and underside are rows of long, stiff, flat spikes. These are like the teeth of a comb, pointing backwards. When a flea is pushed backward, its spikes catch on hair or feathers. It is wedged tight and can't be pushed loose. When the animal stops scratching, the flea just starts walking forward again.

You might also think that a dog or cat's hard claws would squash a flea. But a flea's skin is hard and tough. It's not easy to crush a flea. So, it's difficult for an animal to get rid of fleas!

Actually, a flea doesn't usually stay on the same animal very long. It moves from one animal to another, usually by jumping.

Fleas are amazing jumpers. They can leap as much as 12 to 15 inches (30 to 37.5 centimeters). To match such a jump, a person would have to cover about 700 feet (210 meters) in a single leap!

Most kinds of fleas live on rats, mice, and other animals that live together in nests. A female flea lays eggs on an animal. When the eggs hatch, the young fleas drop off into the nest. They look like white worms, but they are so tiny you can't see them. They eat bits of dead plant and animal food they find in the nest. After a time, they make **cocoons** and become adults. When they come out of the cocoons, they hop onto the nearest animal.

Fleas are tiny insects, but they can be very dangerous. Fleas that live on rats can carry germs that cause terrible diseases. About 650 years ago, some 20 to 30 million people in Europe died from a disease carried by rat fleas. This disease was known as the "Black Death."

The fleas had been sucking the rats' blood, which was full of germs. When the fleas bit people, they passed on the germs. The Black Death, which is now called *bubonic plague (boo BAHN ihk playg),* has struck in many parts of the world. It has killed hundreds of millions of people.

Today, there are ways of keeping bubonic plague from spreading. Most places have programs to get rid of rats and fleas. And where people keep themselves clean and healthy, fleas are not much of a problem.

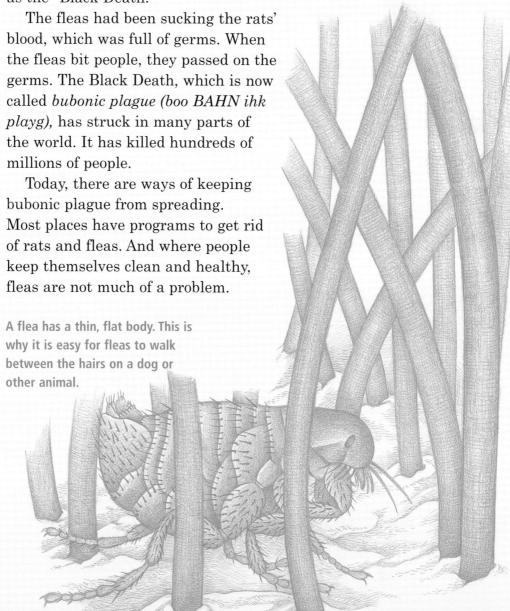

A flea has a thin, flat body. This is why it is easy for fleas to walk between the hairs on a dog or other animal.

Mosquitoes,
Flies, and
Lions

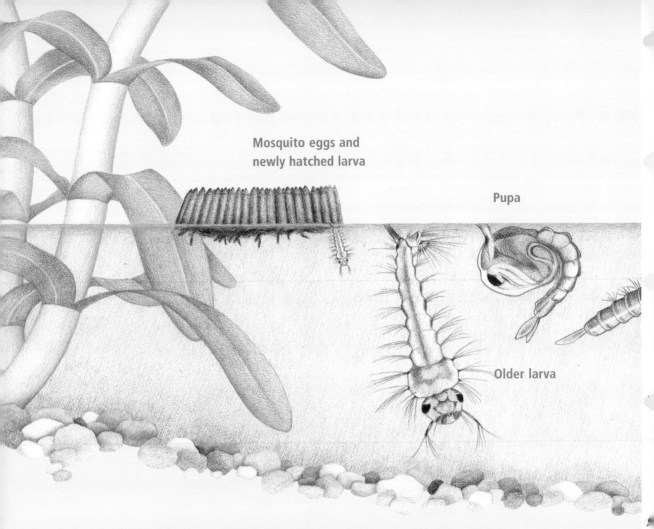

Mosquito eggs and
newly hatched larva

Pupa

Older larva

The life of a mosquito

A cluster of slim, oblong objects floated on the surface
of a small pond. There were nearly 200 of them,
jammed in a tight circle. But the circle was only about
¼ inch (6 millimeters) across. The objects were the
eggs of a single female mosquito *(muh SKEE toh)*.

About two days after the female had laid the eggs,
the first baby mosquito pushed its way through the
bottom of its egg and into the water. It was a slim,
wormlike creature. It had a large, round head with a
dark eye on each side. It had two bushy feelers above
its mouth. And long hairs grew around its mouth.

With quick jerks of its body, the mosquito **larva**
swam away from the circle of eggs. After it stopped

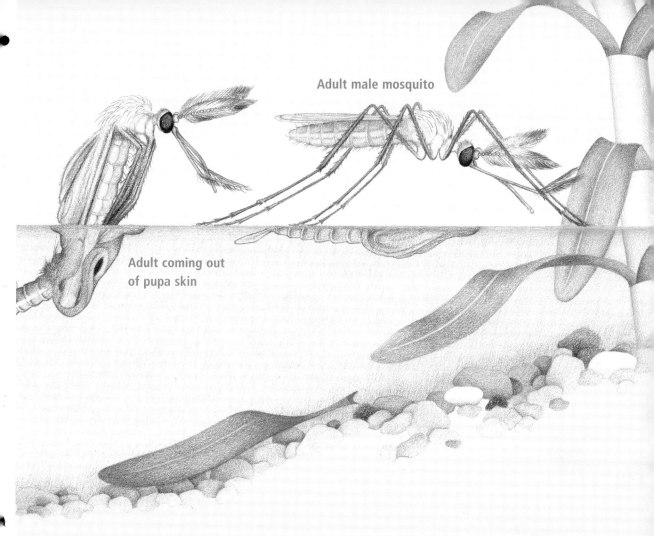

Adult male mosquito

Adult coming out
of pupa skin

swimming, the larva rose backward to the surface of the
water. Poking a tube at the rear of its body up out of the
water, the larva took in air, just as a skin diver breathes
through a snorkel. Then it wriggled down to the bottom
of the pond for its first meal.

The larva ate tiny plants and animals so small you
would need a microscope to see them. Rapidly wiggling
the brushes on its mouth, the larva made currents that
pulled the creatures into its mouth.

The larva was in constant danger. Deadly dragonfly
nymphs lay in ambush on rocks and plants throughout
the pond. Backswimmers sped through the water in
search of **prey.** But the larva survived. For about a week
after it had hatched, it ate and grew. It shed its skin
four times. After the fourth time, it changed into a **pupa.**

The pupa hung just under the surface of the water, its body bent into the shape of a comma. It stopped eating. But, unlike the pupae of most insects, the mosquito pupa could move. Once, threatened by a frog, it dived quickly down to the bottom. Later, it rose to the surface again.

After two days, the pupa's skin split. A male mosquito climbed out. He was a slim, long-legged creature with feathery feelers and two wings. All insects with two wings belong to the fly group. In fact, the name *mosquito* is Spanish for *little fly*.

After a time, the mosquito took to the air. He skimmed toward the edge of the pool and landed on a flower. The mosquito's mouth was a long tube. He poked this tube into the flower and sucked up a meal of sweet **nectar.**

Other mosquitoes soon began to come out of the pond. At first, all were males. Then females appeared. As time passed, the humming of hundreds of mosquitoes filled the air. This humming came from the beating of the mosquitoes' wings, which beat about a thousand times a second.

The next evening, the male joined the other males in a "dance." They flew up in a great swarm. Then, all facing the same way, they rose and fell, rose and fell in the air. Beneath them danced a swarm of females. From time to time, a female would rise up and fly straight among the males.

Suddenly, the "ears" on the male's **antennae** told him a female was heading toward him. He could tell it was a female because the beating of her wings made a higher humming sound than that made by a male. He moved to meet her. Together, they left the dancing swarm and glided downward to mate.

The male lived for only a week after mating. The female had a longer life. Gradually, she wandered farther from the pool. From time to time, she took nectar from a flower. But then she began to feel a need for a different kind of food.

She flew through the woods, searching. Soon, something warm attracted her. The heat came from the body of a flying squirrel on a tree branch. The female mosquito settled on him.

Her mouth was different from that of the male mosquito. Male mosquitoes cannot "bite." But the females can. They have six needle-sharp points at the end of the sipping tube. The female jabbed her tube into the squirrel's skin and sucked up a small amount of blood. Then she flew on.

Much later, she came to a ditch filled with rain water. Skimming down, she laid several hundred eggs on the surface of the water. In the days to come, she'd take more meals of blood and lay more eggs. After about a month, she would die.

House fly

Our worst enemy

What may be the most dangerous animal in the world to people? A shark? A tiger? A poisonous snake? It's none of these. It's actually the common house fly! Why? Because flies carry germs.

Female house flies lay up to 250 eggs at a time, usually on garbage or rotting food. The babies start feeding on the garbage as soon as they hatch. They are tiny, white, wormlike things without legs. They are called *maggots*.

After five or six days, a maggot's skin becomes a thick, brown shell. Inside the shell, the maggot changes into an adult fly with two wings.

Because a fly tastes with its feet, it usually walks all over things "trying them out." In this way, it often gets germs on its feet. If it then walks on people's food, it leaves germs on the food.

Flies also spread germs when they eat. A fly can only suck up liquids. It can also turn some things into liquids. It does this by dissolving them with a liquid it "spits up" from its stomach.

A fly may suck up liquid that has germs in it. This puts the germs into the fly's stomach. If the fly then "spits up" some of its stomach liquid on the sugar at your table, the germs get on the sugar. If you eat the sugar, the germs get into you. So, house flies are dangerous and pesky.

But the flies that come into your house are not all house flies. There are many kinds of these two-winged insects. Many are bothersome, but not all are dangerous. Some are even helpful—they carry **pollen** from one flower to another, helping new plants grow.

Bug Bytes

Repelling bugs that bite!

People have been trying to find ways to repel pesky insects since the time of the ancient Egyptians more than 5,000 years ago! Over the centuries, people have tried to ward off insects with smoke, animal grease, chemicals from plants, and even by eating lots of garlic!

In the 1950's, scientists discovered a compound called *deet* that repelled mosquitoes far better than any other chemical tested. This clear, oily, sticky substance is still the most effective mosquito repellent today. Deet also protects against other blood-feeding insects, including black flies, gnats, chiggers, fleas, and ticks!

A helpful fly

A green caterpillar munched its way along a leaf on a young tomato plant. It would eat for days. After it was finished, the tomato plant might be so damaged it wouldn't produce many tomatoes.

In time, the caterpillar would become a female moth. She would lay eggs. From these eggs, still more leaf-eating caterpillars would hatch. But this caterpillar wasn't going to live to become a moth. A hairy, black fly with a blotch of red on its body had spotted the caterpillar.

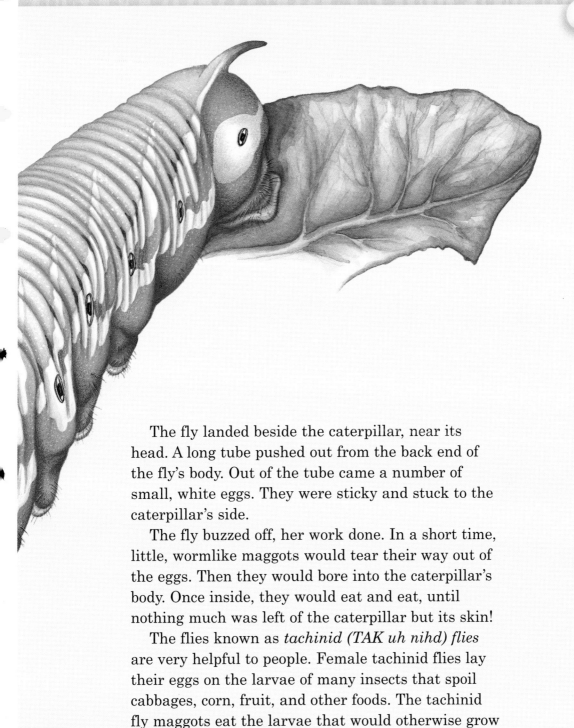

The fly landed beside the caterpillar, near its head. A long tube pushed out from the back end of the fly's body. Out of the tube came a number of small, white eggs. They were sticky and stuck to the caterpillar's side.

The fly buzzed off, her work done. In a short time, little, wormlike maggots would tear their way out of the eggs. Then they would bore into the caterpillar's body. Once inside, they would eat and eat, until nothing much was left of the caterpillar but its skin!

The flies known as *tachinid (TAK uh nihd) flies* are very helpful to people. Female tachinid flies lay their eggs on the larvae of many insects that spoil cabbages, corn, fruit, and other foods. The tachinid fly maggots eat the larvae that would otherwise grow up and lay millions of eggs. These flies are among the best insect helpers we have!

A trap maker

An ant scurried about on a sandy patch of ground. Suddenly, the soft sand slid out from under its feet. It was sliding down the steep side of a pit. It scrambled to try and stop. Then a shower of sand spattered the ant. It lost its balance completely and tumbled to the bottom of the pit.

At once, it was seized by powerful, curved jaws. The ant had fallen into a trap made by an *ant lion!*

An ant lion has a plump, hairy body about 1 inch (25 millimeters) long. Often called a *doodlebug,* it is the larva of a winged insect that looks like a dragonfly.

Soon after an ant lion hatches, it digs a small pit with steep, slanting sides. It starts by walking backward in a circle. (The ant lion can walk only backward.)

The adult ant lion looks like a dragonfly.

It pushes its tail into the sand, like a shovel. The sand slides over the ant lion's flat back, toward its head. When the ant lion jerks its head, it throws up a shower of sand.

The ant lion lies at the bottom of the pit, with its head sticking out of the sand. When an ant or other insect starts to slide into the pit, the ant lion throws sand at it so that the creature will keep sliding. Then the ant lion seizes its prey in its jaws and squirts poison into it. After it sucks the creature dry, the ant lion flips it out of the pit.

In cold weather, an ant lion burrows under the sand to wait for spring. When an ant lion is ready to become an adult, it forms its **cocoon** under the sand. It comes out of the cocoon as a long, slim flying creature with lacy wings.

Spiders and Such

How a spider spins a web

Say "spider" and most people think of a web. Usually, they'll think of what is called an *orb web*. It's the kind people notice because it's pretty. The threads stretch out from the center like the spokes of a wheel. Other threads connect the spokes and form many circles, one inside another.

Suppose you wanted to make a giant orb web, just the way a spider does. You'd need thousands of yards of rope and gallons of glue. You'd also have to climb up and down a rope and walk a tightrope!

The following is not a real activity for you to do. It is just a way for you to have fun as you imagine what a spider's work is like when it builds a web. **Don't really try to do this!**

Imagine this: To begin, you fasten one end of a length of rope high up in a tree. Then you climb down and carry the other end of the rope to a tree about 70 feet (21 meters) away. You climb this tree and fasten the rope so that it stretches between the two trees like a tightrope. (Of course, a spider's tightrope would only stretch between two little twigs. But this is as far for the spider as the distance between the trees is for you!)

Now, fasten another rope to the rope you just attached to the tree. Let this rope hang down to the ground. Slide down the hanging rope and fasten the end in the ground, leaving some slack in the rope.

Next, climb about two-thirds of the way back up the hanging rope and attach a third rope. Holding the end of the third rope, climb all the way up to the tightrope. Carry the third rope back to the first anchor tree and tie the end of it to the tightrope there. Now you have a triangle between the two trees.

An orb weaver builds one of the most
beautiful webs. The silk threads stretch out
from the center like the spokes of a wheel.

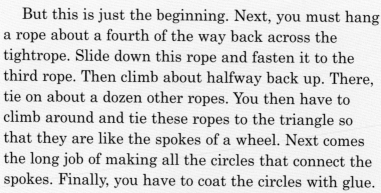

But this is just the beginning. Next, you must hang a rope about a fourth of the way back across the tightrope. Slide down this rope and fasten it to the third rope. Then climb about halfway back up. There, tie on about a dozen other ropes. You then have to climb around and tie these ropes to the triangle so that they are like the spokes of a wheel. Next comes the long job of making all the circles that connect the spokes. Finally, you have to coat the circles with glue.

You can see now what an amazing thing a spider web is, and how hard a spider works to spin one. Some orb webs are 2 feet (60 centimeters) wide. If a spider were as big as an adult, such a web would be about 144 feet (33 meters) wide!

A spider spins its silk "rope" in its body. The silk squirts out of tubes, called *spinnerets,* that are at the back end of the spider's body. The silk comes out as a liquid but dries and hardens as it hits the air. The spider can make either dry or sticky silk.

When its web is finished, the orb-weaver spider hangs underneath the middle of the web or hides nearby. An insect that flies, jumps, or crawls into the web is stuck fast at once. When the insect struggles to free itself, the web shakes. This lets the spider know that something is caught. The spider then hurries toward the trapped insect. An oily liquid on the spider's body and feet keep it from getting stuck in its own web.

The spider uses some of its eight legs to grab the trapped creature. It turns the insect over and over, spraying it with sheets of silk. The insect soon looks like a mummy. Then the spider carries the helpless insect back to the center of the web to be eaten.

A captured insect usually damages the web with its struggles. Some orb weavers repair their web right away. Some make a whole new web after they've caught two or three insects. And others just let their web get ragged and tattered.

A spider spins silk with fingerlike spinnerets on the rear of its abdomen. Liquid silk made in the silk glands flows through the spinnerets to the outside, where it hardens into threads.

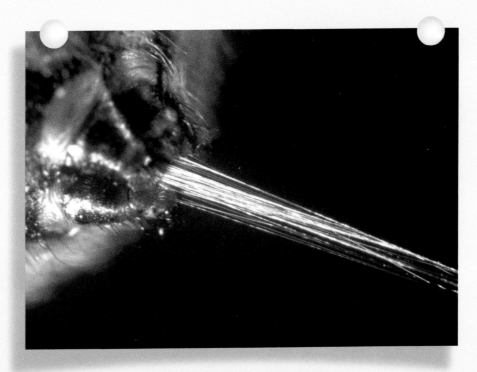

A world of webs

Many kinds of spiders spin webs to catch flying insects. Each kind of spider makes its own special kind of web—from small, sticky traps to large, tightly woven nets. Here are pictures of three very different kinds of webs.

This ladder web (near right) is about 3 feet (91 centimeters) long. Flying moths that bump into it near the top slide to the bottom. There, the spider grabs them.

To catch prey using a triangle web (below), the spider stretches one end of the web tightly. When an insect bumps into the web, the spider lets go. The web folds around the insect.

The filmy dome spider spins a
tangle of threads around a
dome-shaped silk sheet (above)
and hangs under the dome.
Insects that drop onto the dome
are pulled through the webbing
by the spider.

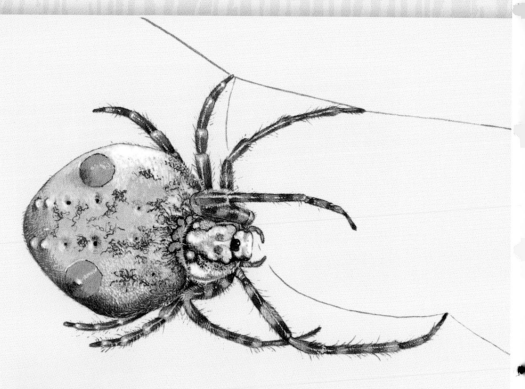

The bolas spider

The fat little spider crouched down, hugging a twig.
All day, as the sun shone on the tree, she hardly moved.
But as the sun finally set and shadows filled the woods,
the spider came to life.

She scurried out onto the end of a branch. There, she
attached a silken thread to the bark with a dab of sticky
silk. Moving a short distance along the branch, she
pasted down the other end of the thread. The thread
now hung from the branch in a loop, like a swing.

The spider crept out onto the thread. She spun
another piece of thread, about 2 inches (5 centimeters)
long. Then she squirted some sticky silk on the end of
the thread to form a gooey ball. Holding this line and
ball with one of her mouthparts and one leg, she waited.

A great many moths and other night insects began to
appear. They swooped and fluttered among the trees.
After many minutes, a moth skimmed by the spider.

At once, she swung her line out toward the moth. The gob of glue on the end struck the moth's body with a plop—and stuck. Desperately, the moth tried to flutter away. But the silk thread attached to the ball of glue held it fast. Quickly, the spider pulled the line toward her, until she was able to grab the struggling moth and give it a poisonous bite.

This little spider that catches insects by throwing a sticky line at them is called a *bolas spider*. A *bola* is a length of rope with a steel ball at each end. South American cowboys use it to catch runaway steers or calves. The weight of the balls makes the rope wind around the animal's legs, so that the animal can't move. The bolas spider's line and ball of glue work in somewhat the same way.

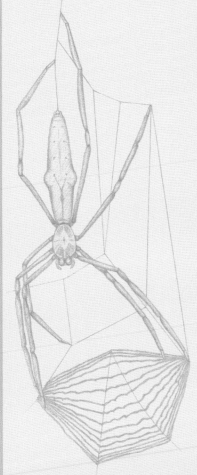

Hunting with a net

The *ogre-faced spider* got its name because of its two huge, staring eyes. These two eyes are much bigger than the spider's other six eyes. They make this creature look like a scary *ogre,* or monster.

The ogre-faced spider hunts in somewhat the same way as a bolas spider. But the ogre-faced spider captures its **prey** with a net!

During the day, an ogre-faced spider stays pressed flat against the bark of a tree. Its thin, brown body looks like a bit of bark. At twilight, the spider moves onto a "platform" of tangled silk threads it has fastened to the tree trunk. Then it spins a net of crisscrossed threads of sticky silk.

The spider hangs by its back legs from its platform or from a silk line. It holds its net in its front legs. When a moth flies near enough, the spider throws itself forward and flings the net over the prey. The net stretches to cover even large moths. Quickly, the spider bites the captured insect and wraps it in silk. Then the spider eats.

Trap-door spiders

Some kinds of spiders live in an underground *burrow,* or tunnel, with a door or lid that opens and closes. The door even has hinges on it!

These spiders are known as *trap-door spiders.* A young trap-door spider digs a tunnel in the earth. It lines the tunnel with silk—like a room covered with thick curtains. Then the spider makes a round door out of layers of dirt and silk. This is fastened to the entrance. The door is quite thick and fits into the entrance like a cork in a bottle.

The outside of the door is made to look like the ground all around the tunnel. When the door is closed, the entrance can hardly be seen. If there is moss on the ground near the entrance, the spider will plant some moss on the door to help hide it.

A trap-door spider sits in the entrance to its burrow, waiting for prey to come near.

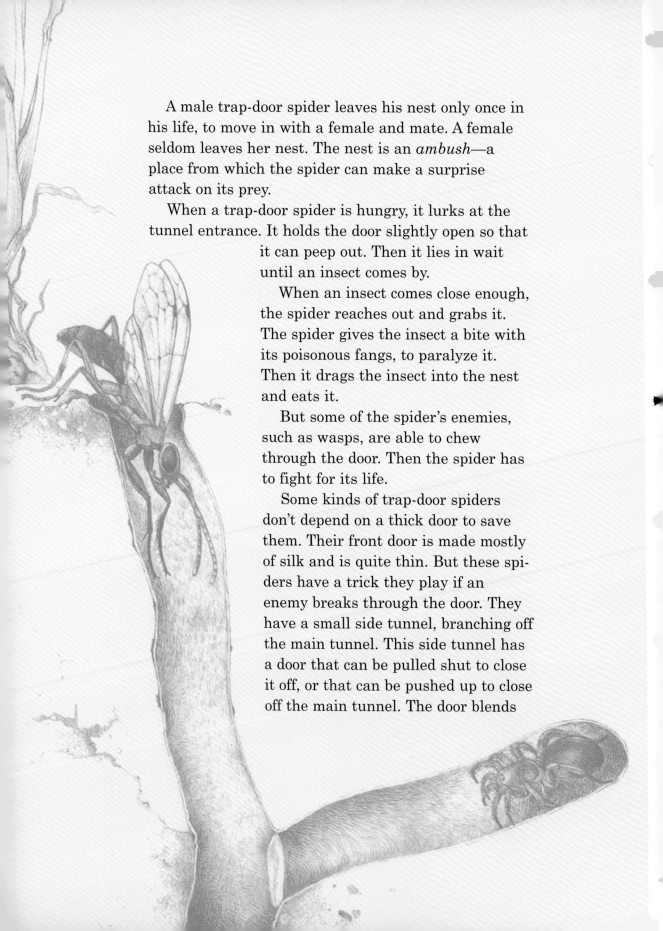

A male trap-door spider leaves his nest only once in his life, to move in with a female and mate. A female seldom leaves her nest. The nest is an *ambush*—a place from which the spider can make a surprise attack on its prey.

When a trap-door spider is hungry, it lurks at the tunnel entrance. It holds the door slightly open so that it can peep out. Then it lies in wait until an insect comes by.

When an insect comes close enough, the spider reaches out and grabs it. The spider gives the insect a bite with its poisonous fangs, to paralyze it. Then it drags the insect into the nest and eats it.

But some of the spider's enemies, such as wasps, are able to chew through the door. Then the spider has to fight for its life.

Some kinds of trap-door spiders don't depend on a thick door to save them. Their front door is made mostly of silk and is quite thin. But these spiders have a trick they play if an enemy breaks through the door. They have a small side tunnel, branching off the main tunnel. This side tunnel has a door that can be pulled shut to close it off, or that can be pushed up to close off the main tunnel. The door blends in perfectly with the tunnel walls. An enemy is often tricked into thinking the tunnel is empty!

One kind of trap-door spider uses part of its body as an extra "door." The spider's back part is very large, hard, and flat across the end. If an enemy breaks down the spider's front door, the spider turns around and goes down its tunnel, headfirst. The tunnel is narrower near the bottom, and the spider's back part is soon wedged in tightly. It forms a thick, hard "door" that an enemy can't bite, sting, or chew through. Finally, the enemy just gives up and goes away!

The trap-door spider makes a door of silk and mud, and attaches it to the lining of its burrow with silk hinges.

Life in a silken tube

A female purseweb spider never sets foot outside her house. She gets her food by pulling it right through the wall!

A purseweb spider's house is partly underground and partly aboveground. The underground part is a deep tunnel at the foot of a tree. This tunnel is lined with silk. The part aboveground is a long tube of silk. This tube stretches up the side of the tree. The tube was named a *purseweb* long ago, because it looked like the kind of purse ladies once carried.

The female purseweb spider spends most of her time inside the tunnel. But she can hear or feel when an insect crawls over her silken tube. She runs "upstairs," inside the tube. She bites right through the silk, sinking her poisonous fangs into the insect. When the insect can no longer move, the spider slits open the wall and drags the creature inside.

After the spider eats, she pushes what is left of her prey out through the slit in the tube. Later, she repairs the slit.

A male purseweb spider lives in much the same way as a female. But males leave home after a time, to look for females. A male wanders about until he finds a tube that belongs to a female. He drums on it with his claws. This tells the female that he is a spider, like her, and not an insect to be attacked.

After a time—when he feels it's safe—the male slits open the tube and goes inside. He and the female mate. Then the male stays in the nest until he dies and the female eats him!

Female purseweb spider

A female purseweb spider waits inside her tunnel for an insect to crawl on the silken tube she has spun.

Dangerous spiders

Most spiders are harmless and even rather helpless. They will almost always scurry out of your way unless forced to defend themselves. Although many spiders have a poisonous bite, the bite of most spiders won't hurt you. However, the bite of some larger spiders can be as painful as a bee sting. And the bite of a very few kinds of spiders can cause pain, sickness, and even death.

The *black widow spider,* which lives in North America, can be dangerous. It often makes its web in the corners of garages, barns, or sheds. The black widow is black with a red mark shaped like an hour-glass on its underside.

The *redback spider,* which lives in Australia, is related to the black widow. This spider is also dangerous. It is black, with a broad red stripe on its back.

Another dangerous North American spider is the *brown recluse (REHK loos* or *rih KLOOS).* It sometimes hides in closets, drawers, or under furniture. It is brown, with a black mark shaped like a violin on its back.

Brown recluse

A black widow spider captures a cricket in its web.

Spider giants!

The biggest spiders are a family of furry, black or brown creatures that live in warm parts of the world. In North America, they are usually called *tarantulas (tuh RAN chuh luhz)*. In other places, they are known as *hairy spiders* or *bird-eating spiders*.

In South America, some of these spiders are large enough to cover a dinner plate! They are hunters. They creep over the ground or through the branches of trees, and leap on their prey. They usually hunt insects, but they also catch and eat birds, lizards, frogs, mice, and other creatures much larger than they are!

Most people are afraid of such large spiders. A few kinds are dangerous, but most are not—their bite is no worse than a bee sting. Some kinds can be tamed and even make good pets!

Bug Bytes

The "spider dance"

Tarantulas get their name from a distantly related wolf spider that lives around Taranto in Italy. People once believed this spider's bite caused a disease called *tarantism (TAR uhn tihz uhm)*. The victims supposedly leaped in the air and ran about making strange noises. According to superstition, the best cure was a lively Italian folk dance that became known as the *tarantella (tar uhn TEHL uh)*.

Flying spiders

The first few days in the life of most spiders are a time of great adventure. Soon after a baby *spiderling* breaks out of its egg sac, it climbs up a tall grass stem or to the top of a bush. Then, facing into the warm spring breeze, it lets out its silken threads.

The breeze catches the strands of thread and pulls the spiderling into the air! Up, up, and away it goes! The bits of thread are like a balloon, which is why this strange sight is called *ballooning*.

How far will the spiderling fly? If the breeze dies, the spiderling may go only a short distance. But it can take off again. By increasing the length of the threads, a spider can go higher. And by shortening the threads, it can come down.

Spiders have come down on ships as far as 200 miles (320 kilometers) from land! And they have been found at a height of 10,000 feet (3,000 meters)!

Why do spiderlings journey through the air? This is nature's way of helping them survive. Hundreds of baby spiderlings come out of every egg sac. If they stayed where they hatched, there wouldn't be enough food for all. By soaring off into the sky, each spiderling has a chance to come down in a place where there are no other spiders.

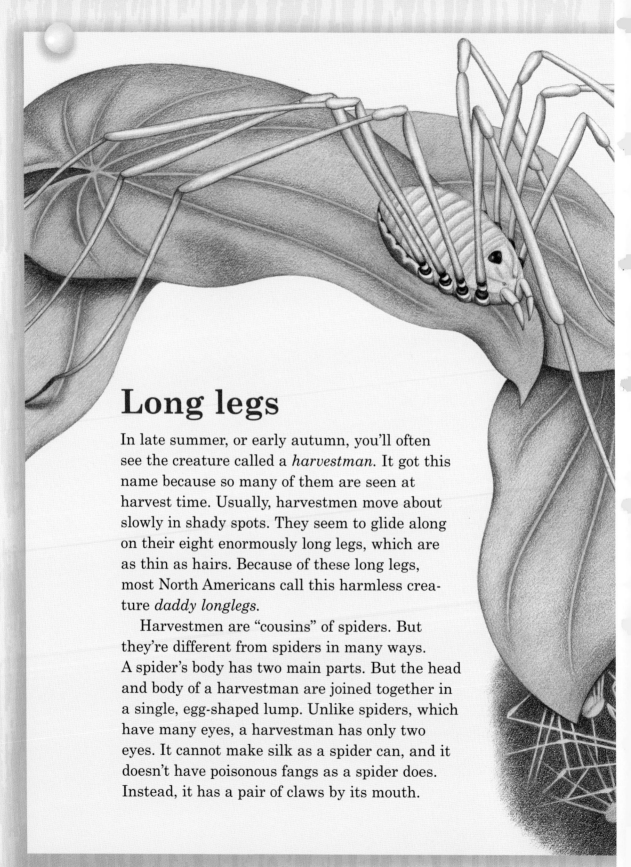

Long legs

In late summer, or early autumn, you'll often see the creature called a *harvestman*. It got this name because so many of them are seen at harvest time. Usually, harvestmen move about slowly in shady spots. They seem to glide along on their eight enormously long legs, which are as thin as hairs. Because of these long legs, most North Americans call this harmless creature *daddy longlegs*.

Harvestmen are "cousins" of spiders. But they're different from spiders in many ways. A spider's body has two main parts. But the head and body of a harvestman are joined together in a single, egg-shaped lump. Unlike spiders, which have many eyes, a harvestman has only two eyes. It cannot make silk as a spider can, and it doesn't have poisonous fangs as a spider does. Instead, it has a pair of claws by its mouth.

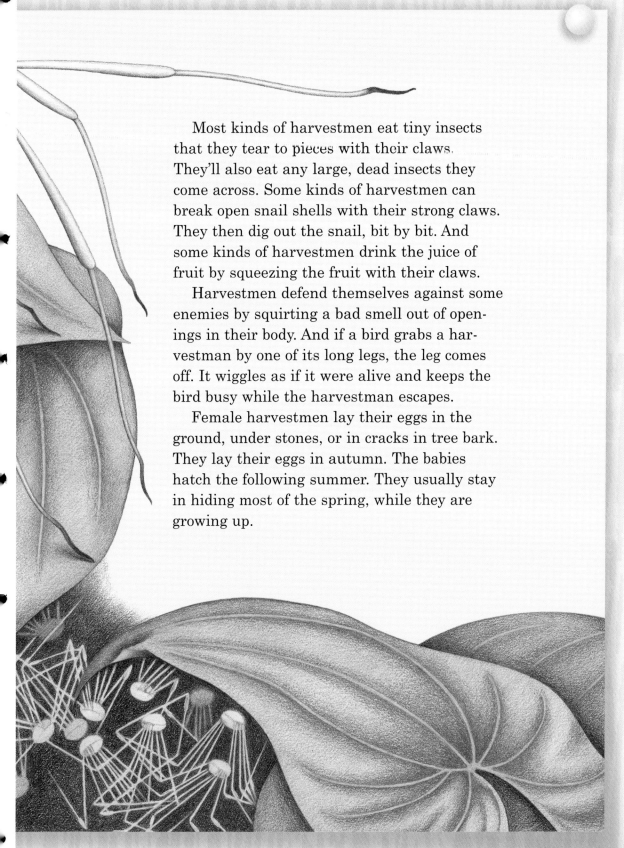

Most kinds of harvestmen eat tiny insects that they tear to pieces with their claws. They'll also eat any large, dead insects they come across. Some kinds of harvestmen can break open snail shells with their strong claws. They then dig out the snail, bit by bit. And some kinds of harvestmen drink the juice of fruit by squeezing the fruit with their claws.

Harvestmen defend themselves against some enemies by squirting a bad smell out of openings in their body. And if a bird grabs a harvestman by one of its long legs, the leg comes off. It wiggles as if it were alive and keeps the bird busy while the harvestman escapes.

Female harvestmen lay their eggs in the ground, under stones, or in cracks in tree bark. They lay their eggs in autumn. The babies hatch the following summer. They usually stay in hiding most of the spring, while they are growing up.

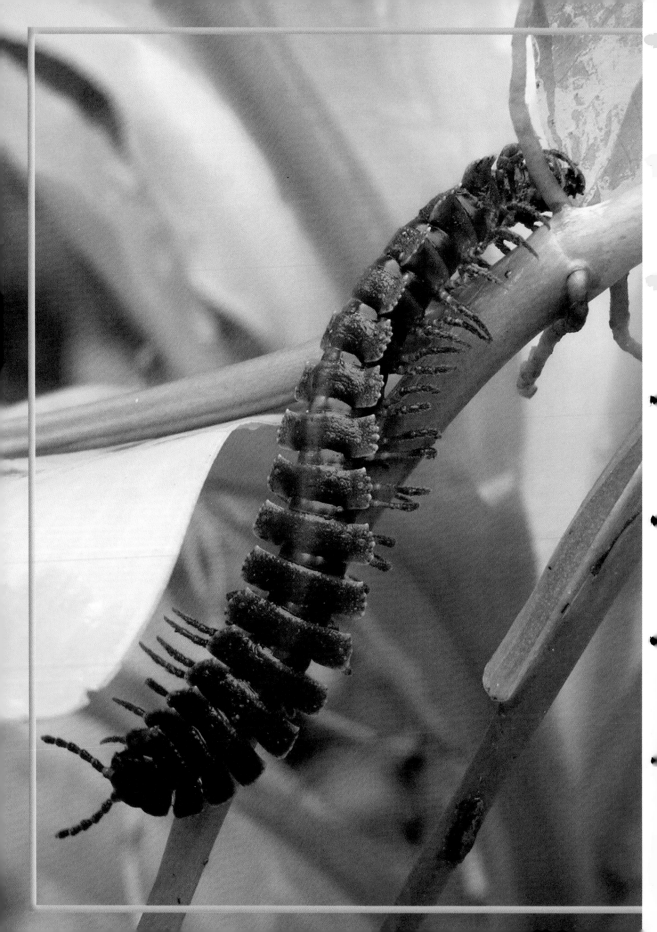

Many-Legged Creatures

"Hundred feet"

The little, wormlike animal lay in the darkness beneath a flat stone. It was the kind of animal called a *slug*. If it could have thought, the slug would probably have thought it was quite safe. What could get at it under the stone?

But another creature was also under the stone. It was a centipede *(SEHN tuh peed),* and it was hunting. With its many feet and long, flat body, it moved quickly and easily in the narrow space. Its feelers jerked and twitched. One of them touched the slug.

In an instant, the sharp fangs on the centipede's jaws stabbed into the slug's body. Poison squirted through the hollow fangs and the slug's life was over. The centipede began to chew.

There are many kinds of centipedes. All are fast, fierce hunters. They hunt in dark places, beneath stones, logs, and piles of leaves. They prey mostly on insect **larvae,** spiders, cockroaches, worms, and slugs.

Most kinds of centipedes are small. But the giant desert centipede of southern North America is very large. It catches birds, mice, lizards, and large insects.

A centipede's narrow body is divided into many sections. Each section has one pair of legs. The name *centipede* means "hundred feet." And some people call these creatures "hundred-legged worms." But almost no centipede has exactly 100 legs. Most have about 70 legs. Some centipedes have only 30, and others have nearly 400!

Centipedes, like insects and spiders, hatch from eggs. Some kinds of baby centipedes look just like their parents. Others have only a few legs when they hatch. Each time they shed their skin, they gain more legs.

One kind of centipede likes to live and hunt in people's houses. Most people try to kill a centipede if they see one in the house. But they shouldn't. A *house centipede* is harmless. And it can be helpful. It will keep the house clean of roaches, flies, silverfish, and other creatures that are harmful.

The giant desert centipede (above) can grow up to 8 inches (20 centimeters) long. Most centipedes are small, such as the house centipede (shown life-sized, right).

Bug Bytes

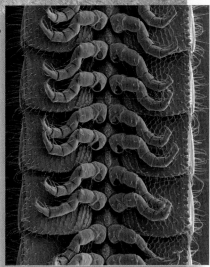

Close-up of legs

Lotsa legs!

In 2006, scientists rediscovered a rare type of millipede that comes the closest to living up to its literal name of "thousand feet"! The creature (above), found only in California, measures about 1⅓ inch (33 millimeters) and has more than 600 legs—more than any other animal alive today!

The rare species was first spotted in 1926 in San Benito County, about 120 miles (192 kilometers) southeast of San Francisco, by a scientist who counted a record 750 legs on the 'pede! Another one of its kind wasn't seen for 80 years, until a scientist spotted one again in the same area of California.

Scientists captured a few of the critters for study. Using a microscope, they found that of those captured, the females were bigger and had nearly twice as many legs as the males had. Some of the female millipedes had up to 666 legs!

"Thousand feet"

Millipedes *(MIHL uh peedz)*, like centipedes, usually live under logs, rocks, and piles of leaves. But their way of life is very different from that of a centipede. Millipedes crawl about very slowly. And they aren't hunters. They eat mostly bits of dead, rotting plants. Some also eat the roots of plants. This causes problems for gardeners and farmers.

Millipedes defend themselves with poison. They give off a smelly liquid that has a stinging, burning, bitter taste. Birds or other animals that try to eat a millipede get a real taste shock. A millipede also has a hard shell, which protects it when it curls up in a circle.

Millipedes come from eggs. Most kinds of millipedes make a nest for their eggs. The female builds

Millipedes are sometimes called "thousand-legged worms." But most types usually have no more than about 300 legs.

a hollow dome out of dirt she mixes with liquid from her mouth. She lays from 20 to 300 eggs through a hole in the top of the dome. Then she seals up the opening and goes on her way.

The young millipedes hatch in several weeks. At first, they have only a few pairs of legs. As they get older, they add more legs.

The name *millipede* means "thousand feet." And some people do call millipedes "thousand-legged worms." But no millipede has this many legs. The greatest known number of legs is about 750.

There are about 10,000 known kinds of millipedes. They live in all parts of the world. But there are probably many kinds of millipedes that scientists have not yet discovered.

Find Out More

Amazing Insects by Koday's Kids at Ivy Hall School, Buffalo Grove, Illinois http://www.ivyhall.district96.K12.il.us/4TH/KKHP/1insects/bugmenu.html

Choose from some 50 insects on the menu and up pop photos and facts about your choice.

Beetles by Kathleen Derzipilski (Benchmark Books, 2005)

Find out how to recognize different kinds of beetles, where they live, and how they grow from babies to adults.

Bug Books by Jill Bailey, Karen Hartley, Chris Macro, and Philip Taylor (Heinemann Library, 2006) 12 volumes

Each book focuses on a different kind of insect, such as centipedes, cockroaches, and ladybugs. Especially helpful are the close-up photos and the diagrams showing the parts of each insect's body.

The Bug Scientists by Donna Jackson (Houghton Mifflin, 2002)

Get to know four scientists who study insects and how they work, and you may come up with some career ideas of your own.

Bugbios by Dexter Sear http://www.insects.org/index.html

This Web site is full of close-up photos of many kinds of insects, especially butterflies.

Bugs and Butterflies by Kaboose http://www.kidsdomain.com/kids/links/Bugs_and_Butterflies.html

Explore the Internet for cool Web sites on insects—from "Antboy's Bugworld" to "Wendell's Yucky Bug World"—all listed in this single Web site.

Bugs – Insects 4 Kids by Ann Zeise, A to Z Home's Cool Homeschooling http://homeschooling.gomilpitas.com/explore/bugs.htm

This resource center has a huge number of links to a wide range of Web sites about insects, listed under such categories as "Bug Arts and Crafts," "Collecting," and "Games."

Classifying Insects by Andrew Solway (Heinemann Library, 2003)

Learn about how scientists classify animals and about the characteristics of each insect group.

Insectigations by Cindy Blobaum (Chicago Review Press, 2005)

The experiments, art projects, and games in this book will draw you deeper into the world of insects.

Insects in Danger by Kathryn Smithyman and Bobbie Kalman (Crabtree Publishing, 2006)

Discover the many insects that are in danger of disappearing, why they are in danger, and what you can do to help save them.

The Life Cycle of Insects by Louise and Richard Spilsbury (Heinemann Library, 2003)

Insects mate, have babies, and grow up to become adults in a variety of ways, which you will see in this book.

A Place for Butterflies by Melissa Stewart (Peachtree Publishers, 2006)

This book examines how 11 different kinds of butterflies help and are helped by the environment they live in.

Spiders by Jill C. Wheeler (Checkerboard Library, 2006) 6 volumes

The six titles in this set look at crab, funnel-web, hobo, recluse, and white-tailed spiders, as well as the spider's cousin, the daddy longlegs.

Young Entomologists' Society (Y.E.S.) http://members.aol.com/YESbugs/outrmenu.html

Join other kids interested in insects in this online club and take advantage of its "Bugs-On-Wheels" program, which maintains a "Minibeast Zoo" and offers workshops and hands-on activities that teach about insects.

Glossary

antenna *(an TEHN uh)* One of the two feelers that most insects and some other creatures have on their head. The plural of antenna is *antennae (an TEHN ee)*.

arachnid *(uh RAK nihd)* An eight-legged animal with a two-part body. Spiders and daddy longlegs are arachnids.

bug A crawling insect with a pointed beak. Bugs use their beaks for sucking and making holes. True bugs are insects that belong to a group called *Hemiptera*.

chrysalis *(KRIHS uh lihs)* A hard shell, or case, that forms around a caterpillar when it starts to turn into a butterfly.

cocoon *(kuh KOON)* A silk covering that many kinds of insect larvae spin around themselves when they are about to turn into adults.

colony *(KOL uh nee)* A group of animals or plants of the same kind that live together.

crustacean *(kruhs TAY shuhn)* A kind of animal that has a shell-covered body and many legs. Crustaceans live mostly in water or damp places. Lobsters, crabs, and shrimp are crustaceans.

drone *(drohn)* A male bee. Drones do not do any work and cannot sting. Their purpose is to mate with a queen, so that she will produce eggs.

fungi *(FUHN jy)* Fungi are living things that do not have *chlorophyll*. Chlorophyll is the green substance that many plants use to make food. Fungi cannot make their own food. They take in food from what is around them. A mushroom is a fungus. The singular of fungi is *fungus. (FUHNG guhs)*.

hive *(hyv)* The name for a place where honeybees live and store their honey. It can be in a hollow tree or log, or it can be a box made by people.

honeycomb *(HUHN ee KOHM)* A wax structure with six-sided compartments called *cells*. Bees make a honeycomb out of wax that comes from their bodies. They use the cells to store honey, pollen, and eggs.

honeydew *(HUHN ee DOO)* The sweet liquid that tiny insects called *aphids* make by sucking juice from leaves. Honeydew drips from leaves in hot weather.

insect *(IHN sehkt)* Any one of a group of small animals with six legs and a body part that is divided into three parts. Most, but not all, have feelers and wings.

larva *(LAHR vuh)* A young insect, from the time it leaves the egg until it becomes a pupa. A caterpillar is the larva of a butterfly or a moth. The plural of larva is *larvae (LAHR vee)*.

migrate *(MY grayt)* To go from one area to another when the seasons change. Some insects and birds migrate.

molt *(mohlt)* To shed old skin, hair, feathers, or other things that grow on the body to make room for new growth. Insects, spiders, snakes, and many other creatures shed their entire outer skin when they molt.

nectar *(NEHK tuhr)* A sweet liquid that is made by many kinds of flowers. Butterflies and many other insects live on nectar. Bees make it into honey.

nymph *(nihmf)* The young form, or *larva*, of an insect that changes directly to the adult stage and then lives on land. It looks like the adult but has no wings or only small wings.

pollen *(POL uhn)* A yellowish powder that is made in the parts of a flower called the *anthers*. When pollen from one flower gets into another flower of the same kind, a seed is formed.

prey *(pray)* Any animal that is hunted or chased by another animal.

pupa *(PYOO puh)* A stage in the development of many kinds of insects. The larva changes into a pupa, which, in turn, develops into an adult.

queen A fully developed female in a colony of insects, such as bees or ants, that lays eggs.

Index

This index is an alphabetical list of important topics covered in this book. It will help you find information given in both words and pictures. To help you understand what an entry means, there is sometimes a helping word in parentheses, for example, **queens** (insects). If there is information in both words and pictures, you will see the words *with pictures* in parentheses after the page number. If there is only a picture, you will see the word *picture* in parentheses after the page number.